HOW TO TRAIN HUNTING DOGS

A trio of Pointer champions pointing chicken (sharp-tailed grouse) on the Canadian prairies
Left to right: Nightcap, Luminary, and Ariel

How to Train
HUNTING DOGS

A SUCCESSFUL SYSTEM OF TRAINING POINTING DOGS,

SPORTING SPANIELS, AND NON-SLIP RETRIEVERS

By

WILLIAM F. BROWN

Editor, THE AMERICAN FIELD

Author of

"The Field Trial Primer," "American Sporting Dogs,"
"Albert Frederick Hochwalt—A Biography,"
"Dogs"—Encyclopedia Americana, 1941 Edition
"Retriever Gun Dogs"

South Brunswick and New York: A. S. Barnes and Company
London: Thomas Yoseloff Ltd

Library of Congress Catalogue Card Number: 70-114858

A.S. Barnes and Co., Inc.
Cranbury, New Jersey 08512

Thomas Yoseloff Ltd
Magdalen House
136-148 Tooley Street
London SE1 2TT, England

Twenty-sixth Printing

ISBN: 0-498-08916-9

Printed in the United States of America

Contents

CHAPTER

Foreword   xi

Introductory   xv

I. Gun Dogs   1

    Pointing Dogs

    Sporting Spaniels

    Retriever Breeds

II. Qualifications to Train a Hunting Dog   6

III. Something About the Pointing Breeds   11

IV. The Sporting Spaniels   27

V. Retriever Breeds   34

VI. Picking the Prospect   51

VII. Important Preliminaries   59

VIII. Implements of Training   67

IX. Early Lessons   73

    Yard Training

    Teaching to Heel

    Teaching to Sit

X. Teaching the Dog to "Whoa!"   84

XI. Coming When Called   90

XII. Introducing the Firearm   96

    Cure of Gun-Shyness

XIII. Early Lessons in the Hunting Field   107

XIV. Lessons in Retrieving   112

XV. Retrieving of Game   124

XVI. Quartering—Hunting to the Gun   134

Contents

CHAPTER		PAGE
XVII.	Telepathic Communication Between Trainer and Dog	143
XVIII.	The Pointing Instinct	149
XIX.	Steadiness on Point	155
XX.	Stopping to Flush or Shot	165
XXI.	Backing	173
XXII.	Undesirable Tendencies and Faults	176
	Pottering	
	Trailing	
	False Pointing	
XXIII.	Blinking, Bolting, Rabbit Chasing	185
	Bolting	
	Handling Pointing Dogs on Fur	
XXIV.	Full Development of Latent Qualities	192
XXV.	Significance of Field Trials	199
XXVI.	Spaniel Technique and Spaniel Trials	204
XXVII.	Recognized Retrievers and Non-Slip Retriever Trials	209
XXVIII.	Dogs for Defense and in War Work	219
XXIX.	Helpful Memoranda	223
	Index	227

Illustrations

Trio of Pointer Champions on Prairie Chicken   *Frontispiece*

PAGE

Pointers—Baconrind and Proctor's Star   xi

Three Pointers and a Setter   xii

Golden Labrador Puppies   xvii

Group of Chesapeakes and a Flat-Coated Retriever   xvii

Spinoni   2

Chesapeake and Flat-Coat   3

Señor J. A. Sanchez Antuñano with Pointers   9

English Setter   14

Irish Setter   16

Gorden Setter   18

Pointer   19

German Shorthair   22

Brittany Spaniel   24

Pair of Brittany Spaniels   25

English Cocker Spaniel   28

Cocker Spaniel   29

English Springer Spaniel   30

Jay F. Carlisle with Labradors   35

Chesapeake Bay Retriever   37

Labrador Retriever   40

Head Study of Labrador   42

Golden Retriever   43

Golden Retriever in Action   43

Irish Water Spaniels   45

Flat-Coat Bringing in Game   47

PAGE

Curly-Coated Retriever   49

Pointer Puppies   52

English Setter Puppies   52

Pointer Puppy Investigating   53

English Setter Puppies Hit the Trail   53

Three-Month-Old Stylist   54

Pair of Pointer Prospects   54

Another Three-Month-Old   55

Pointer Puppies Initiated   55

Pointer Juvenile on Point   56

Youngster Manifests Pointing Instinct   57

Pointing Tendencies   58

Afield with the Yearling   62

A Galaxy of Field Stars   65

Training Aids   68

J.A.S.A. Force Collar   71

Restful Interlude   75

Dog At Heel   78

Pointers "At Heel"   80

Training to Sit   82

Spaniel in "Sit" Position   83

"Sit, Steady"   86

Labrador in "Sit" Position   87

Troupe of Springer Spaniels   91

Irish Setter and Firearms   99

Shooting over Pointers   102

Chesapeakes and Flat-Coat   105

Dog Wagon   108

PAGE

On the Canadian Prairies   110

Forcing dog to open jaws   115

Holding the object for dog   116

Placing object in dog's mouth   117

Dog holding object   118

Setter delivers article   119

Heavier article is substituted   120

Dog approaching with heavy article   121

A double retrieve   125

Cocker Spaniel retrieving rabbit   126

Pointer retrieves dead quail   128

Labrador returning with duck   129

Delivering to hand   130

Holding pheasant   131

Working with Labrador Retrievers   132

Harry D. Kirkover with his dogs   135

The breakaway   136

A pointer and setter search for quail   139

Pointer displays style and intensity   144

Brittany Spaniel with pheasant   146

Setters—Sire and son—pointing quail   150

Pointer on game   152

A lesson with check cord   156

Confirming stanchness on point   159

Advancing to flush birds   160

J. Horace Lytle with Sam Illsley   161

Preparing to confirm stanchness   166

"Whoa, Steady"   168

PAGE

A trio of Pointer Champions . . . 170

Honoring a bracemate's point . . . 174

A pair of field trial winners . . . 177

A scene to delight the hunter . . . 178

A picture to remember . . . 181

A day's bag . . . 183

Prairie training . . . 193

Make a "Buddy" of your dog . . . 194

Hot weather treatment . . . 196

A California field trial . . . 200

The dog wagon . . . 201

Three A. G. C. Sage Pointers . . . 203

Springer Spaniel and Labrador Retrievers . . . 205

Springer Spaniels hurdling obstacle . . . 206

Returning with a pheasant . . . 207

Labrador Retriever . . . 210

Chesapeake Bay dog going to "fall" . . . 211

Chesapeake retrieving pheasant . . . 212

A Labrador at work . . . 213

Labrador Retriever with pheasant . . . 214

Taking to water . . . 216

Labrador Retriever that points . . . 217

FOREWORD

Foreword

A graceful bird dog ranges swiftly through an expansive stubble field, testing each vagrant breeze of the frosty morning for the warm scent of game. Suddenly his rhythmic motion suspends. The dog freezes into a majestic pose, every muscle tense, every fiber aflame, head high and tail aloft. There is character, confidence, *class* in his inspiring attitude. A bevy of bonny bob-white quail is located accurately . . . and the hunter can prepare for some exciting sport.

Just such thrilling moments are making the American sportsman more and more hunting dog conscious. When you go afield to hunt behind a well-trained setter or pointer, you can expect to enjoy that picture many times a day. The thrill has no parallel in recreational sporting activities. And its pulse-stirring quality never dims. Over and over the sportsman can drink in the rich beauty of this striking sporting scene and enjoy the deep emotion that comes with it.

Courtesy American Field, Chicago

Father honoring son's point. A Pair of Pointer Champions—Baconrind, sire, and Proctor's Star

How much, then, is a well-trained gun dog which can provide such stimulating sport worth? As soon as a hunter has become attached to his canine companion, no price can be named. It simply isn't possible to measure in monetary terms the value of such a dog. This is especially true if the sportsman himself has trained the dog.

Then the affectionate bond that exists transcends a king's ransom in gold.

Nothing can give as many thrills, provide as stimulating and beneficial recreation, as hunting with well-trained dogs. The devotee of field sports, particularly upland game bird shooting, is becoming more appreciative of not only the game-finding value of a hunting dog, but is demanding class performance on the part of his canine field companions. During recent years the hunting breeds have gained tremendous popularity and this is our apologia for adding another book to a growing list on the art of training American gun dogs.

Three Pointers and a Setter provide a thrill!

Use of sporting dogs to find, point, and retrieve game has been in vogue for centuries. There has been any number of books written on how to develop properly the natural qualities of the hunting dog and add those refinements of training that assure pleasurable sport afield. Some of these books are better than others, but there is good advice in all of them. The methods advocated or the systems employed are generally sound, to be qualified only by the individual traits, tendencies, and temperament of the particular dog.

It may be said that the use of hunting dogs, especially those which are adept in the art of retrieving, substantially reduces the annual depletion of game birds. This is true because the use of dogs minimizes the number of birds crippled or killed, but unretrieved. Thus a trained gun dog is a mighty important conservation factor.

The majority of books on the training of sporting dogs have limited the text to specialized breeds. The *pointing* breeds, for instance, such as English setters, Irish setters, Gordon setters, pointers, Brittany spaniels, German shorthairs and such other varieties which indicate the presence of game by pointing rigidly the exact location of the birds. The author has undertaken an ambitious assignment in the attempt to cover all the popular breeds of hunting dogs—for there are not only distinctive breed characteristics, but family variations, not to forget the most important individual differences—yet the effort will be made to reduce to as simple language as possible those things the average sportsman who essays to train his dog would like to know.

For in this book the average dog owner, particularly the one-dog owner, will be kept uppermost in mind, the fellow who likes to keep his hunting dog at home for companionship during the off season, and then when the open shooting season rolls around he wants to get out in the field with his loyal canine pal and enjoy some excellent sport. There is an extra something—a greater gratification—if he himself has educated the dog in the art of hunting. It is hoped that this book may be helpful in outlining methods that can be followed successfully in the training of gun dogs.

If perchance the reader has not already acquired a dog, let us caution that if you are going to own a shooting dog, try to own a good one. When making your selection, do not quibble about a few dollars extra cost but endeavor to get a pedigreed puppy likely to develop into the kind of dog you wish. The breed you select depends on the type of hunting you want to do. If you concentrate on upland game bird shooting—quail, ruffed grouse, pheasants, woodcock, prairie chickens and Hungarian partridges—by all means get a pointer or setter. If you want to mix some duck and dove shooting in with your hunting of, say, pheasants and rabbits, likely a spaniel will best serve your purposes. Or if waterfowl shooting dominates your hunting activities with merely an occasional foray for pheasants, consider one of the Retriever breeds—Chesapeake Bay Dog, Labrador Retriever, Irish Water Spaniel, or the other Retriever varieties expert in water work and able to do a real job on land as well.

Unless you are sincere in the desire to train the dog yourself, it is recommended that your dog be placed in the hands of a reliable professional handler for training purposes. To train a *good* hunting dog *properly* is real art. In its highest conception, relatively few have mastered it. This does not mean that the average person cannot achieve entirely satisfactory results. To be perfectly honest, many gun dogs will train themselves. Anybody with patience, persistence, determination, and ability to concentrate can work relative wonders with a dog. Thus if you would like to try your hand at educating your own dog, do not be dissuaded. Keep prominently in mind that while obedience is absolutely essential, the effort should be to *teach* the dog, not just employ *force* for coercion. Intelligent treatment of individual dogs accomplishes the best results. Each pupil may have different characteristics or tendencies which will require special molding. Every successful professional realizes this, and in the application of any effective system of training the temperament of the individual dog must govern.

Actually if you are a fellow who loves to hunt by all means try your hand at training at least one of your shooting dogs. If you will remember the virtue of patience and the success of perseverance, the results of your efforts in gun dog training are bound to give you untold satisfaction.

There may be some material in these pages which the author feels "debunks" what has been said before. Certain recommendations to be made are not in agreement with what other authorities have previously advocated. The majority of these recommendations are the consensus of leading professional sporting dog trainers, men who have made a life's work of educating hunting dogs and consequently are eminently qualified to speak with authority. We are indebted to many noted trainers for their suggestions and assistance, particularly Martin J. Hogan of Barrington, Illinois, whose broad experience in the development and education of gun dogs is unexcelled, and Clyde Morton of Alberta, Alabama, whose record as a handler in the fastest field trial competition for bird dogs bespeaks his superior abilities.

A special word of thanks and expression of deep gratitude to Stewart J. Walpole, Publisher of the *American Field,* whose generous aid in the preparation of this manuscript proved of immeasurable value.

INTRODUCTORY

Introductory

That is the primary question of the prospective dog owner or the novitiate gunner. Unless one has had wide experience with the different breeds, it is difficult to decide just what breed will prove most suitable. It's like buying a new car. Maybe we have been perfectly satisfied with the performance of the make we own and merely get another made by the same manufacturer, without really checking what other cars might be able to do in the way of performance.

Just as certain cars may offer particular features, each of the breeds of gun dogs boast certain characteristics and if one is familiar with such traits, it may dictate the selection of a particular type of dog. It must be stressed, however, that not only are there variations in the different breeds, but individual temperament of dogs is so divergent that one has to consider the peculiarities and idiosyncrasies of the particular dog as much as breed tendencies.

DOG is a mammal of the order *Carnivora*, family *Canidae*. Thus would an encyclopedia describe "man's best friend." It might be added that there are more than one hundred breeds sufficiently dissimilar in appearance to be recognized and named. At some early time man began to breed dogs for particular purposes and with the advance of civilization dogs for different uses were gradually developed. There is little doubt but that dogs for hunting purposes were the first to endear themselves to man. Subsequently, through selective breeding arose types of dogs peculiarly adapted to specialized activity, and these types were ultimately refined into the specific breeds as we know them today.

The American sporting breeds are among the most highly developed of domesticated animals. Any person who has used a gun dog in the practice of sport will acknowledge the remarkable sagacity of the recognized gun dog breeds. There were various groupings of pure-bred dogs in the past, but in the United States at the present time two main divisions are acknowledged—Sporting Dogs and Non-Sporting Dogs. There is a subdivision of the former under the classifications of gun dogs and of hounds. Since in this book we are concerned chiefly with the former, a division made up of gun dogs such as hunt their game by scent but do not kill it, the hounds will not come in for attention, although it might be said that the latter division includes both that class of dogs which hunt their game by scent and kill it—beagles, fox hounds, harriers, et al.,—and the group of sight hunters, such as greyhounds, deerhounds, and wolfhounds.

The Field Dog Stud Book of Chicago, Illinois, the only all-breed registry in the United States which publishes an annual volume of its registration records, recognizes twenty-one distinct breeds in the Sporting Dog Group. In this belong pointers, setters, spaniels, retrievers. Because practically every breed has been developed for specialized activity, the group may be further classified into the specific uses of the various breeds which function much in the same manner, notably those which find and point their game, the types of sporting spaniels which pursue a similar *modus operandi* in the finding and flushing of game in the hunting field, and those breeds which make a specialty of retrieving game.

The American sporting dogs are a development exclusively of the sportsmen and breeders of this country. True, with the notable exceptions of the Chesapeake Bay Dog and the American Water Spaniel, claimed to be distinctively American breeds, the foundations of the various gun dog types are from the British Isles, but through selective breeding and training, the dogs have been developed for, and adapted to, hunting conditions as found to exist in the United States. The evolution of the breeds as we view them today was not accomplished in a day, a week, or a month. It has taken almost a century to develop from English importations the hunting dogs which are currently winning in American field trials. These dogs are bold, independent, endowed with initiative, amazing speed, and wide range, great endurance withal remarkable bird sense and good nose, for these are the qualities a gun dog must possess to be of outstanding usefulness in questing upland game birds in average American coverts. The training of such a dog naturally calls for an understanding of canine psychology and the application of proper technique when confronted by unusual situations. But before going into that, it may be of interest to enumerate the breeds which fall under the various classifications.

Litter of Golden Labrador puppies

A group of Chesapeake Bay Retrievers with a Flat-Coated Retriever

HOW TO TRAIN HUNTING DOGS

Gun Dogs

When we talk about gun dogs, we may mean Pointing dogs, Spaniels, Retrievers. All are of practical value to the sportsman in the hunting field. It might be well to give the individual breeds under each classification.

POINTING DOGS

This group encompasses the oldest and best known sporting dogs in the United States sphere of hunting activity, and they have not only retained their popularity through the years but enjoyed a steady increase in numbers. Falling under this head are:

Brittany Spaniels	Griffons (Wire-Haired Pointing)
English Setters	Irish Setters
German Shorthair Pointers	Pointers
Gordon Setters	Spinoni

SPORTING SPANIELS

The practical use of spaniels in American coverts has come into vogue in relatively recent years, and their rise to the present great popularity has been coincident with the flourishing of the pheasant, for the spaniel has shown extraordinary adaptability in hunting in cover and under conditions where the ringneck thrives. Not only are the spaniels at home in a pheasant environment, but also the gaudy ringneck's tactics of fleeing afoot, running off from the point of a setter or pointer, has many times proved disconcerting to both the dogs and sportsmen, whereas the methods of the spaniels are better suited to cope with the running proclivities of the pheasant.

Spinoni

This is not to say that a smart pointer or setter will not handle the wily ringneck in thrilling and competent fashion, but until a member of the pointing breeds becomes versed in the technique required for successful handling of pheasants, he is not so likely to provide as much shooting as a well-trained spaniel. It might be remarked that beagles have been used on pheasants by some hunters with good results. Under the sporting spaniel classification come:

Clumber Spaniels   Field Spaniels
Cocker Spaniels   Sussex Spaniels
English Springer Spaniels   Welsh Springer Spaniels

RETRIEVER BREEDS

The Retrievers have come into more general use during the last decade, being practically indispensable to the wild-fowler and of marked usefulness to supplement the work of the pointing dogs. It is known, of course, that the Chesapeake Bay Retriever, of Amer-

Left: Chesapeake Bay Retriever; *Right:* Flat-Coated Retriever

ican origin, has had a vogue for many years, chiefly as a waterfowl
specialist, not used very much for land work until the sudden rise
to popularity of the Retriever trials. About a score of years ago,
importations of Labrador Retrievers caused increased attention to
be paid by American sportsmen to the good field performances by
these useful animals when used in conjunction with setters and

pointers. This, with the organization of field trials for the Retriever breeds, accounts for the increasingly large interest now evident in these varieties, which include:

American Water Spaniels	Flat-Coated Retrievers
Chesapeake Bay Retrievers	Golden Retrievers
Curly-Coated Retrievers	Irish Water Spaniels
Labrador Retrievers	

All of these pedigreed sporting breeds have their stanch admirers. Thousands of them are bred and registered each year to supply an ever-increasing demand as more and more hunters realize the effectiveness of a good dog and know that under present conditions use of a dog is essential to find game and avoid tiresome tramping in fruitless quest. That the enjoyment of hunting with well-trained gun dogs, always a favorite pastime of the American sportsman, has increased in popularity steadily over a long span of years can be judged by the number of hunting licenses issued by the various states each year. During the season of 1926-27, more than 5,750,000 hunting licenses for the taking of wild game were issued to sportsmen throughout the United States, a record at the time. Statistics show that 7,646,193 were issued in 1939—an increase of almost two million—with totals in excess of 8,000,000 the last three years.

The relative scarcity of game and the difficulty of finding it induced a higher percentage of these licensees to own and use trained gun dogs, and it has been the aim of federal wild life authorities and state conservation agencies to restock depleted coverts, restore our dwindling game populations, so that the fascinations of hunting may not be lost to posterity. Of course, getting a full bag nowadays has meant that the dogs must be better, the hunters more skillful, and logically extra effort has gone into the breeding, rearing, and training of practical gun dogs.

The author does not pretend to advise just what breed one should own. The selection depends upon the reader, the type of dog he would like to have and to what uses he intends putting him. It is well to remember that the training procedure of the various gun dog breeds follows somewhat similar lines. Indeed, it might be emphasized that each breed can be taught to function throughout the needs of the average sportsman: that is, find and locate game to enable it to be flushed, or sprung, and to retrieve dead or crippled game. Since they are at their best as specialists, however, it is recommended that the breed be selected according to the chief use required. But whatever the sporting breed to be chosen, the important natural qualities to look for in the puppy would be much the same; namely, instinct to hunt; good nose; intelligence; good constitution; nervous energy; good eyesight and hearing; tractable disposition; courage, and good conformation, style and appearance. In the case of the pointing dogs, it is important that the instinct to point be a natural qualification.

CHAPTER II

Qualifications to Train a Hunting Dog

In the preceding chapter the important natural qualities to look for in a gun dog puppy were listed. It is no less important that the person who undertakes the education of the dog be properly qualified. Every author on dog training has said many times, "In order to train a dog, you must know more than the dog." That might well be paraphrased to read, "In order to train a dog, you have to have clearly in mind exactly what you wish to teach him." You have to know definitely what you want the dog to do, and have an intelligent plan of getting him to understand.

The training of a dog embraces for the most part finding a means to communicate to him what you want him to do. A natural medium is, of course, the best way. The comprehension of the dog is limited; while his devotion knows no bounds and he will do everything within his power to please his master, you have to make him understand what is expected of him. But it is wrong to generalize—even about dogs. Just as we have penal institutions for the wayward in our social system, so all dogs do not adhere to the etiquette of the moment. Some are defiant and refuse to respond to a handler's commands, like certain people who defy the conventions of society. Frequently, with intelligent management, this can be overcome, just as in a number of cases wayward persons are rehabilitated and assume a useful place in ordered society. It happens, too, that some of the stubborn dogs with a perverse streak are gifted with amazing aptitude and abundant natural quality; there is a parallel in people. How often have we encountered instances where if a person had chosen to go straight, he could have gained much success in the marts of business, the commerce of states and nations. So it is with

6

bird dogs. Many times we have seen dogs with superlative natural qualities, all the requisites to be topflight winners, but a mean streak, an unstable temperament perhaps, would cause upsets. Trainers, good trainers, have worked their hearts out to make dependable performers of many such a dog, sometimes with success, but just as often failure has resulted. Does this signify the methods employed were wrong? Not by any means. The chances are that the dog's spirit could not be conquered by any training procedure, exactly as we have incorrigibles among criminals. In isolated instances, perhaps, the use of a different training technique might have brought good results, and this is where a trainer of experience has the advantage, for he can take many routes to reach the same destination—obedience and useful performance by the dog. Sometimes force is necessary; sometimes constant association. An owner who makes something of a companion of his hunting dog develops a great deal of intelligence in him as a result of such communion. The companionable relationship of the dog with his owner is in force at a time when his enthusiastic instinctive urge is at rest. The dog's mind is open and the enjoyment he gets out of close association leads him to seek and acquire knowledge. In such cases, many interesting tricks can be taught the dog. When in the field, it is another matter; the dog is all keyed up to follow his hunting desires, and the acquirement of knowledge in the way of obedience that conflicts with his hunting interest is naturally distasteful. One should be careful about making a responsive machine out of his dog in the hunting field, for this may ruin his initiative and seriously curtail his usefulness as a game finder.

Without patience and perseverance, the highest accomplishments in the art of dog training cannot be achieved. You have to possess good old-fashioned stick-to-it-iveness in order to be a successful trainer. What's more, training implies keeping a dog in condition. What would some of our greatest natural athletes be without a trainer to keep them in the pink of condition. All of our major league baseball teams and collegiate football squads have "trainers," men who are retained for the express purpose of keeping each member of the squad in the best possible physical shape.

It should always be remembered that the health, diet, and care of your dog are of utmost importance. By an observance of elementary points, such as regular and careful feeding, clean drinking water, a daily brush and plenty of exercise, a dog carries with him an atmosphere of contentment, and he is the performer which will give you consistently the best that is in him. The hunting dog should not be given only part time attention. It isn't enough to consider him only during the open shooting season. He deserves your best efforts in his behalf at all times and in return will more than repay you with loyalty, devotion, companionship, and provide thrilling recreation and excellent sport in the hunting field.

Keep your dog comfortable and physically fit. Competent veterinary service is now generally available and there are authoritative books on feeding and care which go into these aspects of dog ownership more thoroughly than can be done in this work. But make it a point to be sure that your gun dog is well fed, that his diet is a balanced one, providing all elements and vitamins necessary for growth, maintenance, and procreation. Keep him in condition and give him a preparatory period prior to any actual shooting expedition afield. Don't expect your dog, after a long summer layoff, to be able to go out and hunt all day. Give him short workouts, for, as has been inferred, conditioning is just as important to your dog's performance afield as spring training for major league baseball players or a pugilist's activities in training camp before a big boxing bout.

The love for a good dog is natural enough with most men and this coupled with a hunting urge is ample qualification for any person to undertake the training of his gun dog. Decide what kind of dog you want, make up your mind definitely as to what you wish him to do—*then go to it,* remembering always that patience, kindness, and perseverance are indispensable virtues.

It is notable that some handlers prove more proficient in the development and training of dogs of a particular breed or of a certain temperament. This is because such handlers have greater aptitude along well defined lines or because their methods are suited to the mental qualities, courage, capacity, etc., of the breed, or the type of temperament ordinarily found in dogs of that particular strain. The development of highly strung, finely bred bird dogs, where nothing desirable must be taken from the dog in the process of training, requires great skill and proper use of approved methods. This means allowing wide latitude for the unhampered development of the natural qualities of the dog, at the same time bringing him

Señor J. A. Sanchez Antuñano, originator of the J.A.S.A. System of Gun Dog Training, guns over a pair of his Pointers

to an acceptable point of subservience to the gun without sacrifice of his initiative or impairment of his independence. The fiery, brilliant performer cannot be subjugated in the same manner as a phlegmatic plodder; dogs differ in temperament as much as people and these differences are not confined within strict breed lines. While it isn't safe to generalize when talking about dog temperament, or peculiarly identify with a breed individual reactions, it may be stated that in the case of retrievers, greater force can ordinarily be exercised, so that a man lacking the finesse, the patience, and the versatility of, say, a successful trainer of setters and pointers, may get good results—and in less time. Even choosing between the greater bird dogs, the pointer will as a general thing stand more punishment than the setter, but the person who aspires to train his dog must remember that kindness, patience, and firmness, never indiscriminate punishment, get best results. Mere mechanical performance can be achieved by using force to coerce obedience, but the experienced handler frowns upon this for the proper training of a gun dog means full development of natural qualities and potentialities, plus a strengthening of character, not mere mechanical response.

Anyone who has read this far may begin to doubt his abilities and now consider the job as one to be tackled only by an experienced professional. But if you ask the question, *"Can I train my hunting dog myself?"* the answer will be an unequivocal—ABSOLUTELY, *if* you will take the time and trouble. The trainer will have to make sacrifices, concentrate on his task, exercise rigid control of his own temper and emotions, and be fully prepared to see it through. It is not the purpose of this book to make training a gun dog seem a complex thing, too hard for the ordinary person. The aim is to make it as easy as possible and avoid any long list of things to do and not to do. However, marvelous results in dog education are achieved only by dint of intelligently directed effort, patient perseverance, and a clear idea of what the dog is to do.

The successful dog trainer really has only one formula. We are going to strip all the hocus-pocus from it by giving it to you in a single sentence. *Make the dog understand what you want him to do.* It is seldom indeed that one encounters a dog that will not do his utmost to please his master if he knows what is expected of him!

But dog training is not as simple as its formula is concise. The person who seeks to train his own dog will be confronted by numerous problems. If he will be patient, if he will be kind though firm, if he will get on intimate terms with his dog and endeavor to understand canine psychology by studying the dog's normal reactions, if he will strive intelligently to make the dog understand what is wanted, success will crown his efforts.

Each dog is an individual case. Mass education of dogs is all right to the same extent as mass education of children. You can give certain phases of yard training to a whole group of dogs all at once just as a teacher instructs a class of pupils. But the instructor who best prepares his students for a place in life is the one who studies the requirements of the individual and seeks to impart useful knowledge in a way that the particular pupil can absorb it most readily.

The purpose of this book is to help the trainer, especially the novice. All systems of training have considerable good in them and certain methods have proved successful in literally thousands of instances. The course of training set forth in these pages is that followed by noted professionals, and it is hoped that the reader will gain serviceable knowledge of how these expert trainers coped with the various, and sometimes perplexing, situations with which they were confronted.

CHAPTER III

Something About the Pointing Breeds

In the realms of hunting, there are numerous specialized purposes for which dogs are employed. For many of these uses, particular breeds are physically and instinctively extraordinarily well adapted. For instance, pointers and setters excel naturally as bird finders, with a predisposition to point their game. Certain breeds are more proficient in retrieving—from the time the puppies are able to waddle, the recognized Retrievers do it. The Spaniels adapt themselves readily to particular purposes. It must always be kept uppermost in mind that the individuals of the various breeds differ greatly— some require less education than others because they have extraordinary aptitude. Natural qualities are what every experienced trainer looks for!

True, almost any dog can be taught to do definite things. Look at the range of different tricks learned by dogs of various breeds. Nevertheless, the fact remains that certain breeds have a natural bent for a particular purpose—specialists, indeed—and the wise thing to do is select a member of a breed designed for the particular purpose the sportsman has in mind when he considers buying a dog.

It has been emphasized that one should not haphazardly choose the particular breed. Fundamentally, the type of work the dog will be called upon to do should dictate your preference. If you want him principally for upland game birds, better decide on a pointer or setter. If the dog is to fulfill the functions of a spaniel, the springer is most popular with practical sportsmen, although the working qualities of the Cocker are extolled by its admirers. Or if you desire a retrieving specialist, a Labrador, Chesapeake or other breed of Retriever should be the choice. Decide first of all what you will expect the dog to do, then pick out the breed best suited to fulfill your wishes. But do not indiscriminately select the individual dog. This is of real importance. It is preferable to have the assistance of an experienced "dog man" or trainer when making the selection. There are a lot of things to know if you want to pass expert judgment upon a dog, and you won't get all that knowledge out of this book—*or any other*—but because it is believed that it might be helpful to state briefly something about the origin, development, and uses of the popular sporting breeds, the various gun dogs will be discussed with a view to giving the unsophisticated sportsman a bit of knowledge of the background of each breed plus presentation of a succinct standard. It is deemed desirable to do this before entering upon the methods of training hunting dogs—the successive stages of development to make your canine field companion a shooting dog par excellence.

We are not the first to say that the origin of the dog, domesticated carnivorous mammal remarkable for its intelligence and its attachment to man, is shrouded in obscurity. Many theories have been advanced about how the dog originated—none entirely satisfactory. As far back as the dog is found represented by drawings, paintings, sculpture, or carvings, he is depicted as a distinct animal. A few writers, cloaking their remarks in language brilliant as a diamond solitaire and as authoritative as a sheriff's badge, have insisted that the dog is but a wolf, or a jackal, domesticated. These authors really know no more about the dog's exact ancestry than others who ascribe to the dog credit for originality, as in the case of other animals. As a matter of historic fact, originality of the dog would be as easy of establishment as some of the bizarre theories still presented in reference to the genesis of "man's best friend."

It is not essential to our purposes to delve into the speculative part of dog history. We do know that clear evidence of the existence of the dog as used for hunting has been found in the Egyptian tomb of Amten, who ruled during the Fourth Dynasty, somewhere about 3500 B.C. And to come quickly to the gun dog breeds with which we are today familiar, let us consider first the pointing dogs, best known and most popular.

SETTERS

Any history of the setter must commence with its evident spaniel ancestry. The consensus among writers of canine literature, past and present, is that the setter is an improved spaniel, or, as Edward Laverack put it, "A spaniel improved." There is some conjecture, nevertheless, for in early writings are statements that the setter was originally produced from crosses of the Spanish pointer, the large water spaniel and the Springer spaniel, consequently it may be that Bernard Waters arrives close to the truth in "The American Book of the Dog" when he says in effect that the origin of the setter, like most other breeds, is obscure and all theories advanced are nothing more than guesswork and theoretical speculation.

Most modern authorities accept as fact that the "setting spaniel" was the forerunner of today's setter and that the setter breeds were developed in Great Britain. The three varieties—English setter, Gordon setter, and Irish setter—were developed individually, and depicted as distinct breeds as early as 1805. Although fanciers of each have contended that their type were the aborigines, there is no evidence to substantiate which claim is just. Taking for granted that the long-legged spaniel, or setting spaniel, originally used for netting purposes, was gradually developed to range and to stand his birds for the net, it has not been established definitely which of the three distinct varieties we know today came first, albeit a majority of canine historians adhere to the belief that the Irish setter deserves rating as the purest.

Setters became prominent as gun dogs about 1775, and by careful cultivation attained a high degree of proficiency in finding and pointing game, particularly in open country. All three of the modern breeds of setters utilize similar technique in hunting: the dogs are fast, graceful in action, range boldly, possess superior scenting powers, detect the presence of game by scent or the effluvia of the quarry, and indicate the location by establishment of a stanch point with nose pointing in the direction of the game. Setters make quick, dependable, tender-mouthed retrievers. Now for treatment of each breed.

Taking up the actual history of the making of the English setter, there is little doubt that the major credit for the development of the modern setter should go to Edward Laverack, author of "The Setter," a resident of Whitchurch, Shropshire, England. Mr. Laver-

Courtesy American Field, Chicago

English Setter

ack, through a remarkable process of inbreeding, was responsible for the development of the type which was not only the standard of excellence in his day (1815-1900), but the type upon which has been builded the present day English setter. The Laveracks provided foundation stock for the strain known as Llewellin setters. The Field Dog Stud Book records the members of the English setter breed which trace without an outcross to Duke-Kate-Rhoebe-and-the-Laveracks as "Llewellins." While straight-bred Llewellins enjoyed their greatest vogue about 1900-1925, the strain retains its popularity with many setter breeders.

The Laverack setter, so-called, was a strain unequaled in its day. Although the pedigree records published by Mr. Laverack have been openly questioned, the fact remains that he developed a tribe which proved of great importance in promoting breed improvement. Subsequently the late R. Ll. Purcell Llewellin of Pembrokeshire, South Wales—like Laverack, an Englishman—used Laverack blood principally in his breeding operations to establish the strain which bears his name. English setters (chiefly of Laverack and Llewellin blood) imported from England were combined with select "native" American stock to produce the modern English setter, or American setter as some designate it, which is now acknowledged a superior hunting dog to either the Irish setter or the Gordon setter. The English setter and the pointer are today's favorites in bird dog trials.

A mild, affectionate disposition is characteristic of the English setter, along with beauty, intelligence, and aristocratic appearance. The dog is parti-colored, white generally predominating, height at the shoulder from twenty-two to twenty-five inches, weight ranging from thirty-five to sixty pounds when conditioned for field work, albeit the typical bench show setter is a more cumbersome specimen, carrying extra avoirdupois and seldom boasting the marvelous muscle formation of field trial setters. However, as in the case of race horses, it may be said that good field trial dogs "run in all shapes and sizes."

The English setter is the most popular of the three setter varieties. The dog is bred principally for utility purposes and the breed has enjoyed great success in bird dog trials. The standard for the English setter calls for a long skull with well defined stop and a long, fairly square muzzle, straight and not dished. Moderate length ears, carried close and set well back and low. The chest should be of good depth and the back straight and strong. Good bone in the legs; feet closely set and with tough pads. Coat moderately long and flat, showing thin feathering on the legs. In motion the individual should suggest gracefulness of movement and endurance.

The English setter is a mighty competent bird dog. Because of his coat, longer than the pointer's, enabling him to withstand lower temperatures, he enjoys greatest favor in the north, and his coat is also a protection against punishing cover. For questing quail, pheasant, ruffed grouse, prairie chicken, Hungarian partridge—all of the popular upland game birds—the setter is capable of proficient performance, and the hunter may expect pleasing results accompanied by many thrills.

THE IRISH SETTER

The Irish setter, a stylish individual, beautiful of coat, of handsome conformation and commanding appearance, has long been beloved, albeit his use as a hunting dog has not been so great as that of his English cousin during the last thirty years. The Irish setter first

Irish Setter

came into popular notice early in the eighteenth century and less than a hundred years later his reputation was firmly established, not only in his native Ireland but throughout the British Isles. Speculation as to his exact origin is little more than guesswork, various breeds having been named as his progenitors. Today the breed standard calls for the color of an Irish setter to be a rich golden chestnut or mahogany red (with small white markings on chest, throat or toes permissible), whereas in Ireland the earliest ancestors were chiefly red and white, the white frequently predominating over the red, and even today many individuals across the water are particolored. In the United States, however, solid reds—or reds with inconspicuous white markings—are the only ones accepted as typical.

Because of his distinctive appearance and rich mahogany coat, the Irish setter has been bred more for show purposes than for field work, particularly during the last third of a century, consequently the breed does not rival successfully with the pointers and English setters in the current field trials. Indeed, it is seldom that an Irish setter competes in the leading trials, although many sportsmen still prefer to use the red dog for gunning purposes. The Irish setter hunts and works similarly to the English setter, not so fast in action nor so bold in range, but gifted with a good nose, stanchness on point, and he is a desirable gun dog. Individuals of the breed, taken as a whole, are somewhat larger and heavier than the English setter.

THE GORDON SETTER

The Gordon, or black and tan setter, is a representative member of the bird dog family, but the breed is not known so well in America as either the English or Irish setter. The variety originated in Scotland, but it is doubtful if the breed came into existence, as its name would imply, at the Castle Kennels of the Duke of Gordon. That His Grace was partial to black and tan setters and bred them extensively in the latter part of the eighteenth century is an established fact, but it is also known that half a score of wealthy Scottish sportsmen were doing the same thing at the same time, and even earlier. But the prominence of the Duke reasonably explains the choice of name to identifying the breed.

The forebears of the Gordon setter were much the same as those of the other two varieties already described. In general appearance the Gordon loses little, if anything, by comparison with his rivals in the bird dog field, although his color militates against his use in coverts, making him difficult to see because the black and tan markings do not contrast with surrounding foliage. Indeed, the English setter, with white predominant, is more conspicuous in the field than either the Irish red setter or the Gordon black and tan setter, and this in a measure accounted for the greater popularity of the English setter for hunting and field trial purposes and resulted in subsequent outstanding development of his field qualities.

Some sportsmen claim that for cover shooting, where a dog must work at close quarters, the Gordon setter has no superior. His disposition is to cover the ground slowly, but thoroughly, though he possesses attributes similar to his setter cousins. While not quite so high at the shoulder as a typical Irish setter, the Gordon gives the impression of strength and stamina, of sturdy construction with

Gordon Setter

adequate bone. The only permissible color is black with tan markings on the legs and underparts, the border lines between the black and tan colors clearly defined. The Gordon setter has never risen to widespread popularity in America.

THE POINTER

It is commonly believed that the pointer came originally from Spain or Portugal. Authorities are not agreed on this. Some insist that the breed was known in England before the importation of the dog termed the Spanish pointer. However, it is generally conceded that the pointer varieties found in Spain, France, Germany, and Italy, and in England, too, were originally of some old stock which had been known throughout eastern Europe, and were trained for use as gun dogs in keeping with the process of development of the gun.

The pointer comes by his name honestly, because so long as we

Pointer

have any accurate record he was the first dog to stand—or point— game in the precise sense that the term is used today.

The first pointers of which there is any dependable record appeared in England about 1650. As early as 1711, Gay, in his poem, "Rural Sports," wrote in a way that indicated a well-known and thoroughly established fact:

> "See how the well-taught pointer leads the way:
> The scent grows warm; he stops, he springs the prey;
> The fluttering coveys from the stubble rise,
> And on swift wing divide the sounding skies;
> The scattering lead pursues the certain sight,
> And death in thunder overtakes their flight."

The pointer unquestionably evolved from a type of hound—foxhound, greyhound and bloodhound, with the inevitable "setting spaniel" infusion—the dog being used for finding purposes and subsequently developed to fulfill his present function as a gun dog.

Many writers subscribe to the belief that the heavy, strongly-built Spanish pointer was doubtless the chief progenitor of the pointer of the modern day and that in breeding for a faster dog, perhaps both foxhound and setter crosses were resorted to. But it stands to reason that the process of selection of individuals, the use for breeding purposes of lighter, better built and faster dogs, contributed most to the establishment of the breed as it is known today.

Pointers hunt upland game birds by body scent principally. When the dog approaches near enough to game, he stiffens into a stanch point and holds this attitude until the hunter arrives and flushes the birds, the trained performer remaining steady to wing and shot. Many pointers are also taught to retrieve the birds after the game is shot. The inclination to stand motionless on scenting game is a proud heritage of the pointer, developed through years of training his ancestors.

Perhaps some early fanciers went beyond the pale for outcrosses, using different breeds with their pointers, but when the public stud books were established experimental crosses with alien blood were abandoned and the pointer matings kept within pure breed lines. Signal importations to America from England were made along about 1870-1890, the pedigrees of these dogs being authenticated for several generations. From Price's Bang, Mainspring (and his son, Jingo), and King of Kent (plus his son, Rip Rap), the modern American pointer sprang.

The pointer, a shorthaired dog with the capacity for early development, possessed of the competitive spirit in high degree, gifted with speed, range, endurance, and nose, has become the favorite of professional bird dog trainers, and the growth in popularity of field trials has unquestionably brought the breed into greater prominence than ever. Pointer technique in hunting parallels that of the setter, but when it comes to training there is a variance in the disposition of the two breeds. The pointer develops more quickly and his education can be forced without dire consequences. The setter needs more time and added tact is required in his training.

The standard for the pointer describes a dog which is swift and merry in action, symmetrical, about the same size as the English setter—in height and weight—with a short coat. Owing to the shortness of his coat, the pointer is peculiarly adapted to hunting in the South. The setter has an advantage in brush country or in briery growths, or in the North where the temperatures are generally lower. Where burs are prevalent, the pointer enjoys an advantage with his short coat, because the burs so readily adhere to the setter's silky hair. However, there is little to equal the grace and elegance of a classy pointer or stylish setter in action afield. The pointer, so far as numbers are concerned, rivals the English setter. The Field Dog Stud Book of Chicago registers about 7,500 of each breed annually.

THE GERMAN SHORTHAIR POINTER

This breed was developed in Germany and hailed as the "every-use" dog. During the seventeenth century, 'tis said, the Germans imported from Spain individuals of the old Spanish pointer breed, primarily for use as pointing bird dogs. While the Germans liked the Spanish pointer as a bird dog, they determined later that what they needed was a dog which would point birds and rabbits during the day and trail other animals at night. Accordingly, they crossed the Spanish pointer with the bloodhound. The result of this cross was a heavy dog that pointed upland game birds and did a workmanlike job of trailing after dark.

It is undoubtedly true that the German Shorthair pointer was bred to attain all-around performance, good on upland game birds, satisfactory on rabbits and hares, plus ability as a waterfowl retriever. With the growth of popularity of field trials, there was an infusion of the agile American pointer to streamline the conformation of the Shorthair. The standard, by the way, approves a dock-tail.

The breed has gained a measure of appreciation since introduced into America in the 1920s, and a number of representatives of this breed have started in field trials, but ordinarily when compared with pointers and setters the Shorthair is generally slow, circumscribed in range, lacking the independence, initiative, and high flight of foot that we have come to expect in our American bird dogs. Although field trial competitions have not displayed the qualities of the German Shorthair to advantage alongside of setters and pointers, this has not deterred enthusiastic fanciers of the breed from hailing their type of gun dog as a paragon of aptitude and adaptability. They claim the Shorthair came into popularity because of its ability to supply a growing demand for greater adaptability,

German Shorthair

and that in this "all-purpose" dog there is wrapped in a single hide, its admirers boast:

1. A stanch-pointing bird dog
2. A keen-nosed night trailer
3. A proved marsh dog
4. A natural retriever, on land or water
5. Pleasing conformation and markings
6. Great powers of endurance
7. An alert family watch dog and
8. An intelligent companion

The reader can take it or leave it. But on the basis of our experience, the German Shorthair has a long way to come to rival the excellence afield of setters and pointers.

WIRE-HAIRED POINTING GRIFFON

It is seldom that you see a griffon in the hunting field any more. But thirty or forty years ago an esoteric group praised the qualities of this breed and, while the griffon's popularity never became widespread, the breed gained quite a reputation for its hunting prowess.

The Wire-Haired Pointing Griffon is of Dutch origin, tracing back to the 1870s. E. K. Korthals, son of a wealthy banker in Holland, is recognized as the father of the breed, the development of which occurred principally in France, where the dog was known as Korthals' griffon.

The late Louis A. Thebaud of Convent, N. J., sponsored the griffon in America, importing specimens from France early in the 1900s, and through Mr. Thebaud's energetic promotion the breed achieved considerable fame for its keen nose, pointing qualities, and retrieving ability. The griffon is not a handsome individual gauged by pointer and setter standards, for his wiry coat and scraggly mustachioed face would not get him far in a beauty contest. But he is a sturdy if deliberate workman, content with slow pace and almost gun-shot range. The griffon is claimed to possess endurance to a marked degree. He points his game and is said to be a strong swimmer and an excellent water retriever.

A dog about 20 to 24 inches in height, fairly short back, a trifle low on the legs, but strong limbed, his general ensemble indicates strength and vigor. His coat is harsh like the bristles of a wild boar and the appearance, even of those with the short coat, is unkempt, though the facial expression does not lack for intelligence. Admirers of the breed insist that the griffon can be trained to hunt and handle any game.

BRITTANY SPANIEL

Many readers may wonder why this dog is considered with the pointing breeds rather than in the spaniel classification. Simply because the Brittany hunts and points his game in the manner of the setter and the pointer.

The Brittany, the only pointing spaniel, is a relatively recent addition to the Sporting Dog Group in America, hailing from France where he has been a popular gun dog for a good many years—centuries, in fact. True to his name, he came originally from Bretagne, or Brittany. While he points his game like setters and pointers, he is indubitably of true spaniel ancestry, having been bred up to his present height—18 to 20 inches at the shoulder—from original spaniel size. He bears some resemblance to the springer, though longer legged but not so heavy in bone. The ears of the Brittany are shorter and his coat not so dense. Predominating colors are

Brittany Spaniel

white and orange, and white and liver, with various shades such as lemon, mahogany, chestnut, etc.

If asked to describe the Brittany, it would be fitting to say that in appearance it is in between the English setter and the springer, with ears set higher than the setter's, a rather pointed muzzle although a really snipy nose is frowned upon. The tail of the Brittany is naturally short, about four inches. The first tailless ancestor of the modern Brittany spaniel was bred about a century ago at Pontou, a modest town situated in the Valley of Douron. Tailless Brittany spaniels appear occasionally.

The pointing instinct has been developed to a high degree in the Brittany. Used widely on the continent of Europe, the Brittany has since 1931, when the first specimens were imported to the United States, come into some popularity in America. The number of Brittany spaniels competing with pointers and setters in American field trials has been growing. Several field trials are held for this breed alone.

A pair of Brittany Spaniels

Ordinarily of slower pace and somewhat restricted range, the Brittany is not a rival of the pointer or setter in major field trial competitions, but in shooting dog events representatives of the breed have won laurels when opposed by these better known and more numerous breeds. In France, some sportsmen made a practice of referring to the Brittany as "an old man's gun dog," supposedly descriptive of the comfortable pace and modest range of the dog, making it easy for an elderly person to follow the Brittany afield. But ardent supporters of the breed in the United States will brook no contradiction of their claim that the Brittany's pace has been stepped up and that it is the most adaptable of the gun dogs with extraordinary powers of scent. It might be noted that the Brittany can be trained to retrieve very easily and he enjoys such work. Besides, he is of a nice size to carry in a passenger automobile.

It is interesting to note that the late Louis A. Thebaud, who introduced the Wire-Haired Pointing Griffon to this country, likewise played a leading role in Brittany importations. Dr. Chester Henry Keogh of Chicago, Illinois, has been among the more successful breeders of Brittanys in the United States, while Jean Pugibet of Mexico City, Mexico, has produced a number of outstanding representatives of the breed.

CHAPTER IV

The Sporting Spaniels

Spaniels have been used for hunting purposes for over five centuries. It is generally accepted that the spaniel derives his name from Spain, and most probably we are indebted to breeders of that country for much of the blood in many of our sporting breeds of today. The first knowledge of the spaniel, according to James Watson in "The Dog Book," is obtained from the work of the French count, Gaston de Foix, who in 1387 wrote his book called "Livre de Chasse." In that work the author brought out that while the spaniel owes its name to Spain, whether it originated there or whether it was bred from dogs which came with the early migrations from the East, will never be known.

From the spaniel, specifically the setting spaniel, was developed the setter of today. But there were evolved other varieties of spaniels, depending upon the individual fields in which these breeds were used. At this time the Clumber, Cocker, English Springer, Welsh Springer, Field, and Sussex spaniels are listed. There is no getting around the fact that the spaniel family is a large one.

The spaniel method of hunting is to quarter the ground ahead of the gun, covering all territory within ordinary shooting range; this properly is done at a fast, snappy pace. Upon flushing game, the spaniel should immediately stop or "hup," assuming a sitting position so as not to interfere with the shot. He is expected to retrieve only on command. The spaniel worker should be under control at all times as there is nothing that can spoil so many shots as an unmanageable dog. Spaniels are valuable for water retrieving; practically all of them take to water readily and are natural retrievers.

The Irish Water Spaniel has not been mentioned, because it comes properly under the Retriever Breeds.

COCKER SPANIEL

The Cocker spaniel is the most popular breed in America to-day. On the basis of pure-bred dog registrations made during recent years, the Cocker is indeed the most popular pedigreed dog the

Typical English Cocker Spaniel

United States has ever had. Over 25,000 were registered in accredited American stud books during 1941!

Very few of these dogs—indeed, too small a percentage—are used for field work. In fact it seems that American breeders have not been concerned with the Cocker's capabilities as a worker. The versatility of this serviceable dog, the smallest of the sporting spaniels, is not appreciated or enjoyed by many fanciers who favor the breed exclusively for bench show purposes or as a house pet and companion. The Cocker can fill the latter roles to perfection, but he ought not be denied his natural vocation of hunting. He is by nature a gun dog and his working attributes should not be overlooked or ignored. Besides, his size makes it easy to carry him to shooting places; his cheerful disposition, merry manner and effective work are features that endear him to everyone familiar with his excellent qualities.

The Cocker is not so robust as the Springer; his maximum standard weight is 24 pounds. It should be noted that many fanciers with sporting proclivities have urged somewhat larger proportions for the Cocker, and there is no gainsaying that the merry little fellow could be bred up to carry out the hunting chores for which he is suited without infringement on the sphere of usefulness occu-

Courtesy American Field, Chicago

Cocker Spaniel

pied by the larger spaniel types. The Cocker must be small enough to penetrate thick undergrowth, but sufficiently high on the leg to carry a pheasant or fair-sized rabbit.

In the game field the Cocker hunts in the approved spaniel manner. A general description of the breed is that of an alert, serviceable-looking little dog, with an expression of great intelligence. Possessed of a sturdy body, powerful quarters and strong, well-boned limbs, he should nevertheless impress as being a dog capable of considerable speed combined with endurance. Quickness, merriness, with an air of alertness and a carriage of head and stern suggestive of an inclination to work, are desirable characteristics. His coat should be flat or slightly waved, silky and very dense, with ample setter-like feather. Color, solid or parti-color.

Any one familiar with the temperament and character of the

"merrie little Cocker" is an admirer of the breed. This is true despite the fact that the Cocker is the most temperamental of the spaniels. Bull-dozing tactics do not go with the development and education of the Cocker; rough-shod training methods are taboo; to get his full confidence and compliance requires sympathetic understanding—time, patience and gentleness, as well as firmness, on the part of his human tutor.

Field trials for Cocker spaniels were started in the United States in 1924. There has been increasing interest in the sport and field use enthusiasts have been the foremost advocates of increased stature for the American variety, which is on the somewhat lighter side in comparison with the English Cocker spaniel.

ENGLISH SPRINGER SPANIEL

The English Springer Spaniel Field Trial Association states that the name "Springing Spaniel" was originally occupational in its nomenclature and generic in its application. That is to say, "spring-

English Springer Spaniel

ing" defined the method of the dog in the hunting field to flush game, while the term included in one broad classification the ancestral stock from which most, if not all, of our present-day land spaniels emanated. It was in 1902 that the Kennel Club of England recognized the English Springer Spaniel as a distinct breed.

The Springer ranks next to the Cocker in popularity, but relatively a larger number of Springers are used for hunting and for retrieving purposes than the doughty Cocker. Sometimes the two breeds compete in the same stakes at spaniel trials, because their methods of working are similar. Field trial competitions for Springers in the United States, it may be interpolated, began shortly after the organization of the English Springer Spaniel Field Trial Association in 1924.

The Springer employs typical spaniel technique in the hunting field. He is a sturdy dog, endowed with the speed, agility, and endurance to cope with the most difficult hunting conditions. Considerably larger than the Cocker—his weight may be almost twice as much—the Springer is active, symmetrical, strong, but not ponderous. He is approximately 19 inches at the shoulder and males may weigh as much as 45 pounds. He is unquestionably the most widely used of the land spaniels in hunting upland game birds and also sees much service in waterfowl shooting. The Springer is the favorite of many nimrods, he is especially serviceable in the quest of pheasants, very useful as a retriever on land and from water area, and owners of large plantations in the South frequently use a team of Springers to supplement the work of pointers and setters, the spaniels doing all of the retrieving.

WELSH SPRINGER SPANIEL

Although not so well known as the English Springer Spaniel, the Welsh Springer Spaniel is much admired by those familiar with his excellent qualities. Although the Welsh Springer is somewhat smaller than the English Springer, the principal difference is that the former is always red and white—the one and only color of the Welsh, whereas the English Springer may be several hues.

The Welsh is a very keen sporting dog with a superior nose and ability to withstand extremes of heat and cold better than most dogs. He has marked endurance and when trained properly is a most useful gun dog. Hobart Ames of Grand Junction, Tenn., president of the National Field Trial Champion Association, uses Welsh Springers to retrieve the bob-white quail shot over his pointing dogs.

CLUMBER SPANIEL

Deriving its name from Clumber Park, the estate of the Duke of Newcastle, this is an extremely heavy-bodied animal quite distinct from other members of the spaniel family. It is easy to identify the Clumber as a spaniel, but he is more massive in appearance and more phlegmatic in his movements than the more streamlined, agile, snappy Springer and Cocker. The Clumber is decidedly more popular in England than here—in fact, there has been few importations, the dog, slow moving and deliberate, being much better suited to shooting conditions over there than is the case in American coverts where game is scarce, and the bustling, fast-moving spaniel preferred.

We remember one of the Clumbers brought to the Middle West a few years ago—a big, cumbersome, massive spaniel, yet quite impressive in appearance, dignified, plodding, but withal a sure-nosed individual and a capable retriever. Besides his physical conformation, the Clumber is easily identified by his color, which generally is almost entirely white with few lemon or orange markings, the less markings the more typical. He may tip the scales at as much as 65 pounds.

SUSSEX SPANIEL

This breed has not been imported heavily to the United States. It was developed in England, has an extremely fine nose, but lacks the speed of the Springer and Cocker, nevertheless is a determined hunter and a valuable shooting companion. Lack of popularity in America may be attributed to the fact that the Sussex Spaniel does not possess sufficient speed for the average American sportsman, in this respect resembling the Clumber. The conformation of the Sussex—back and loin long and very muscular, legs very short and strong—points towards a slow-moving dog. The breed is inclined to give tongue on scent.

The purity of the breed is indicated by the invariable color, rich golden liver. Weight range is from 35 to 45 pounds. The Sussex is not difficult to train and retrieving is one of his accomplishments.

FIELD SPANIEL

This breed was also developed in England, passing through many exaggerations of type before being brought to the useful and handsome breed we know today. Usually black in color, the Field Spaniel is of symmetrical proportions, good balance of height for length, and he is of a type admired by all who like Sporting Spaniels. His evolution embraced repeated crossing of Sussex and Cocker spaniels. He comes nowhere near approaching the popularity of Cockers or Springers, but fanciers of the breed extol his endurance, speed, and nose. Level-headedness, intelligence and perseverance are breed characteristics. The Field Spaniel stands about 18 inches at the shoulder and the range in weight is 35 to 50 pounds.

CHAPTER V

Retriever Breeds

The Retriever breeds are specialists. They have been evolved to fulfill an important function in the hunting sphere and there is no dispute that these breeds are without a peer in their particular activity. To name the recognized Retrievers—breeds included are Chesapeake Bay Retrievers, Labrador Retrievers, Curly-Coated, Flat-Coated and Golden Retrievers, Irish Water Spaniels, and American Water Spaniels.

In England it is common practice to use a non-slip Retriever to supplement the work of the pointing dogs. But the American sportsman familiar with the versatility of our bird dog breeds may question and even scoff at the necessity of a regular Retriever. You often hear a pointer or setter owner claim heatedly, "My setter (or pointer, as the case may be) is excellent at retrieving, likes to do it, and does it faster than a ponderous Lab or a cumbersome Chesapeake."

This writer does not intend to start any argument on the proposition of superior retrievers. Certainly, setters and pointers can be taught the retrieving art—we intend to tell how later in this book—and this added accomplishment makes them more proficient gun dogs. Properly trained, they can do a first-class job of retrieving. But it isn't the primary purpose of these breeds to retrieve. Searching for, finding, and pointing game—that's their mission in life—whereas the recognized Retrievers make a life's work of bringing dead and crippled game to hand. Although it is easy enough to teach setters and pointers to retrieve, it is no longer a requirement in field trial competitions, hence few dogs in the public eye are versed in the art, though many owners still boast of the retrieving prowess of their shooting dogs.

The Retriever, as has been said, is a specialist, and should not

Courtesy American Field, Chicago

The late Jay F. Carlisle with a double team of Labrador Retrievers

be called upon to find game for the gun. His proper work is always after the shot. It is known, of course, that Retrievers can be taught to search for, locate, and flush game in the manner of the spaniel, but this is not ordinarily required of the Retriever breeds. The function of a Retriever on upland game (fur or feather) is to walk at heel or remain on the line until ordered to fetch dead or crippled game, the "fall" of which he should be qualified to mark. Thus, while the Retriever has nothing at all to do with the actual finding of live game when employed solely as a retriever, he is called upon to mark where the killed or crippled game falls. When given the order to retrieve, he must seek the "fall" in a brisk, quiet manner, thoroughly quartering the immediate area around the fall without unnecessary disturbance off the line of fall. The dog should fetch on command only, then return to heel until given further orders.

When working on waterfowl, a Retriever's place is in the blind until actually ordered to go out. He is expected to note the fall of ducks and sometimes in the process of retrieving a duck is required to mark several dead or wounded ducks at the same time, delivering each in turn, returning for the unretrieved fowl until all have been brought to hand. It is remarkable the way, when several ducks may be downed, a Retriever first goes after a bird that is crippled and brings the dead ducks in afterwards, apparently reasoning that immediate capture of the cripple is desirable—that the dead birds can wait! Of course, if a cripple is in sight his struggles may attract the dog, but on blind retrieves some canines seem to sense instinctively when a bird is only wounded.

Some men who carry a shotgun in the field may not realize just how tough a job the Retriever has, but veterans appreciate what trying tasks he is called upon to do. The Retriever must proceed quietly with the hunter, yet be alert to mark the fall of game dropped by the gunner. Walking along slowly at heel is mighty trying for any keen hunting dog; the Retriever would be immediately condemned if he romped like some of the other gun dog breeds to work off excess energy before settling to his allotted task. He has to be docile, but constantly alert for he will be called upon to accomplish difficult as well as easy retrieves with marked effectiveness. There will be more said about the working qualities of the Retriever in later chapters, but now for a brief consideration of the distinct breeds.

CHESAPEAKE BAY RETRIEVER

The Chesapeake has been the apple of the American wild-fowler's eye since recognition of the breed. Of truly American origin, the increasingly large interest in the other varieties of Retrievers has not impaired the popularity of the Chesapeake Bay with sportsmen familiar with the superior qualities of this sturdy companion. The Chessy has long been celebrated as an extraordinary water dog, widely known for ability to bring in ducks, and Retriever trials during recent seasons have demonstrated that to his aquatic abilities the Chesapeake has added improved qualities as a land worker.

Courtesy American Field, Chicago

Chesapeake Bay Retriever

The breed boasts a romantic background. The history of the Chesapeake, while never completely authenticated, traces the breed origin to a pair of Newfoundland puppies, a dog and bitch, rescued off the Maryland coast. According to tradition, about the year 1805 there arrived at Baltimore a ship called the "Canton," which while at sea had met with an English brig bound from Newfoundland to England. The brig was in a sinking condition and the crew and some of the cargo were rescued by the American vessel. The cargo included the pair of puppies, presumed to be Newfoundlands, the dog seal brown in color and the bitch, black. The puppies were presented to a Mr. Law, who had extended hospitality to the wrecked sailors. The dog was named Sailor, the female, Canton, and Sailor passed into the hands of Governor Lloyd of Maryland, while the bitch became the property of Dr. Stewart of Sparrows Point, Md. The pair earned great reputations as water workers and in consequence many of the nondescript dogs then being used for retrieving in that area were bred to them, the progeny eventually becoming formally recognized as a breed; viz., Chesapeake Bay Dogs. It is presumed, though there is no authentic record, that Sailor and Canton were mated together.

It took a hundred years and more to fix biologically the breed. Some claim that outcrosses of English otter hounds were resorted to, but this has never been established, nor has the more likely claim that Flat-Coated and Curly-Coated Retrievers were used as outcrosses been substantiated. But the origin of the breed is definitely American and the result of the development of the Chesapeake, as might be expected, is a dog distinctive in type and of high efficiency for the purpose in view.

The type evolved is big and powerful—the ancestors had to be to gain fame for their prowess in the icy and rough waters of Chesapeake Bay, where the dogs were frequently called upon to retrieve a couple of hundred or more ducks in a single day. This required miles of swimming in ice-cold water with perhaps a half-dozen dives thrown in on some retrieves. Bone, muscle, sinews were not enough; the Chesapeake of old needed heart, an indomitable spirit. The power, spirit, stamina, courage, willingness to work, love of water, nose, intelligence, and disposition of those early Chesapeakes which gained renown in the early '80s, are reflected in the modern members of the breed, a proud heritage.

The breed standard calls for a well proportioned dog, nicely balanced, with good head properties, a muscular neck, powerful shoulders, deep chest, body of medium length with back quarters as high or a trifle higher than the shoulders. Hind quarters should be especially powerful to supply the driving power for swimming. Tail should be of medium length; coat thick and short, with a dense fine woolly undercoat; a curly coat is not permissible. Any color varying from a dark brown to a faded tan. Solid color is preferred although a white spot on breast and toes is permissible. The maximum height for males is 26 inches and weight approximately 75 pounds.

In disposition the Chesapeake is most extraordinary. He is quiet but does not like to be disturbed, especially while watching over a stool of decoys. But he is not vicious or quarrelsome with either dogs or people. He simply prefers to be left alone. It seems that to the Chesapeake life begins and ends retrieving and tolling for ducks —or retrieving upland game. The late John F. Parks wrote concerning these grand dogs:

"The Chesapeakes have been developed to a very high state of perfection on the shores of Chesapeake Bay and have been used as retrievers by duck hunters in that locality for many years. In color the dogs range from a deep seal brown to a very light sedge or 'faded buffalo' color, and in coat from the smooth, wavy, short coat to the heavy, thick coat resembling the sheep pelt. These dogs have what is known as the double coat, the under coat being thick and furlike, while the outer coat is of coarse hair.

"The thoroughbread Chesapeake is absolutely fearless and was never known to quit under the most trying circumstances. Deep mud, tangled rice beds and brushes, as well as extreme cold, has no terrors for him. In order to be in a position to fully appreciate these dogs, one must come in actual contact with them and enjoy their companionship. They are, without doubt, the wisest dogs in existence, and as companions they are simply in a class by themselves. As a rule, they are what is known as 'one-man' dogs. That is, they recognize but one master, and when they are properly trained to retrieve, an owner need not worry about getting his own duck when shooting with others on a marsh or on a river."

We have simply quoted Mr. Parks and do not hold any brief for his claims. Fanciers of other gun dog breeds are just as earnest in their recitation of the working qualities of the type they favor.

LABRADOR RETRIEVER

Labrador Retrievers have sprung into great popularity in the United States within the last decade. They have good noses, are adapted to general work with the gun, and have proved superior water dogs, hardy and persevering in the retrieving of waterfowl. The Labrador's coat is close, short, dense, and free from feather.

In appearance the dog gives the impression of being compactly constructed, possessed of great strength and agility. The "otter tail" is a distinctive breed feature.

The Labrador Retriever was introduced into England by the 2nd Earl of Malmesbury. The breed did not originate in Labrador, as the name implies, but in Newfoundland. The Earl happened to see one of these dogs in a fishing boat early in the nineteenth century and arranged to have some of them sent to England. The reputation of the breed as admirable retrievers preceded it, and the smooth-coated dog was said to have been preferred in Newfoundland—"because in frosty weather the long-haired kind become encumbered with ice on coming out of the water."

Labrador Retriever

As the Labrador Retriever Club points out, the dogs were not at first generally known in England as Labradors, but it is accepted that Colonel Hawker, a noted British sportsman, had reference to the breed when in 1830 he mentioned what he called the St. John's breed of water dog. "This type," said the Colonel, referring to what is now known as the Labrador, "is by far the best for any kind of shooting. He is generally black and no bigger than a pointer, very fine in legs, with short smooth hair; is extremely quick, running, swimming, and fighting. . . . Their sense of smell is hardly to be credited: in finding wounded game there is not a living equal in the canine race."

Colonel Hawker was unfamiliar with the breed being developed in the Chesapeake Bay region along about that date, now known as the Chesapeake Bay Retriever, and for which early supporters made claims similar to what the Colonel said about the Labrador. In short, as was pointed out previously, you can get involved in a great many arguments if you go out on a limb with a declaration of all-around superiority for any particular breed of Retriever. We merely recite the fact of known breed history, perhaps even quote claims of admirers of the particular type, but it is up to the reader to interpret these as he wishes. We can tell you about standards, natural qualities, and methods of training, but frankly would not attempt to influence your taste. Each breed has much to recommend it. Because it is now possible to witness the recognized Retriever breeds in competition at public trials in various parts of the country, any sportsman wishing to make a choice may well attend these tests and judge for himself.

Getting back to the Labrador Retriever, there is an external calmness about the dog that radiates confidence in his ability to do what is desired of him. A serenity of disposition that makes the Labrador an excellent companion. Ordinarily he is not temperamental; in fact, even those dogs which exude great keenness and fire, outwardly are imperturbable and seemingly seek to learn only what the master requires, then endeavor to do the job thoroughly, expeditiously.

Supporters of the Labrador Retriever claim for him greater fleetness of foot in land work than the other breeds of Retrievers, and public trials have demonstrated the justness of such a claim. The Labrador is also especially swift in the water and has plenty of stamina, though his endurance as a swimmer may not parallel the phenomenal perseverance of the Chesapeake.

While it is said that in England there was interbreeding with other types of retrievers during the early days of the breed's development, Labrador fanciers put a halt to this by drawing up a standard to discourage any outcrossing. Today the Labrador Retriever breeds very true to type. His weight will average between 60 and 70 pounds, height at shoulder approximately 22 inches, and while the standard permits any whole color, it is generally solid black. Solid yellow Labradors are increasing in popularity. It may be remembered that early in the 1930s, Chesapeake supporters made a great to-do about the color of the Chesapeake blending with blind surroundings, whereas the solid black Labrador coat would make that dog easily visible to ducks, thus keeping waterfowl out of range. This may have induced some sportsmen to take up the yellow Lab.

Be that as it may, when a novice looks over a litter of jet black Labrador puppies, he is at a loss to see how the various youngsters can be distinguished, identified individually by the owner, because they are likely to appear to the unpracticed eye as much alike as so many peas in a pod. It is notable that in England no Labrador Retriever can be designated a Bench Champion until he has qualified in the field, and has been awarded a certificate on the merit of his working qualities.

Labrador Retriever

A distinctive feature of the breed is the tail and the standard states that "it should be very thick towards the base, gradually tapering towards the tip, of medium length, should be practically free from any feathering, but should be clothed thickly all around with the Labrador's short, thick, dense coat, thus giving the peculiar 'rounded' appearance which has been described as the 'otter' tail. The tail may be carried gaily, but should not curl too far over the back."

More and more sportsfolk are using Labradors to supplement the work of pointers and setters on upland game birds. This has been the practice for years in England, but is just gaining favor on this side of the Atlantic.

GOLDEN RETRIEVER

Here is a breed that has made rapid strides in the United States during the last five years. Much of this increased popularity may be attributed to the excellence of the performances rendered by out-

Golden Retriever

standing Golden Retrievers in public field trials in various parts of
the country. Sportsmen have noted the superior qualities and de-
pendability of these successful Goldens, thus it is only natural that
broadened interest in the breed has resulted.

The Golden Retriever, as a sporting breed, dates back just short
of a century. The forerunner of the Golden was a larger dog known
as the Russian tracker, dogs that served a variety of purposes in

Golden Retriever

Asiatic Russia. One of the principal uses of the Russian tracker was as a shepherd dog. He was considerably larger than the modern Golden, approximately 30 inches at the shoulder and frequently weighing as much as 100 pounds, whereas physically the Golden of today compares with the Labrador Retriever, a range of 55 to 70 pounds in weight and about 24 inches maximum at the shoulder.

Sir Dudley Marjoribanks, the first Lord Tweedmouth, while visiting a circus at Brighton, England, in 1860, acquired a troupe of eight dogs from a Russian trainer. The intelligence displayed by these animals made Sir Dudley envision their excellence in the hunting field. The members of this original circus canine troupe, bred without outcrossing for a decade, are recorded as the founders of the Golden, although to establish the breed as it is known today, these dogs subsequently were crossed with the bloodhound. This caused a reduction in size, presumably promoted an intensification of scenting powers, and brought a refinement in the texture of coat.

The Golden Retriever made his initial appearance in the United States just prior to World War I, but interest in him flagged until the early 1930s. Appreciable progress, as intimated, has been made in the last ten years. While in England the Golden has been used frequently as a combined game finder and retriever, its forte is retrieving, and on this side of the Atlantic the breed has been used almost exclusively for retrieving purposes. The Golden is equally at home on land or in water. The breed's pace in land work has been gradually accelerated; a decade ago the Golden was consistently outpaced by the Labrador, but has improved in rapidity of land work and is endowed with plenty of staying qualities when it comes to aquatic abilities. Distinctive breed features are the rich golden coat which must be flat or wavy, with an undercoat dense and water resisting.

IRISH WATER SPANIEL

In spite of the implications of its name, the Irish Water Spaniel is more correctly considered with the recognized Retrievers, for the strong point of this tallest of the spaniels is retrieving waterfowl. A rather strange looking critter, this "clown" of the spaniel family, and even its stanchest supporters would not bet on the prospects of the Irish Water Spaniel in any contest of canine pulchritude.

The peculiar appearance of the Irish Water Spaniel doesn't defy

A group of Irish Water Spaniels "On Dress Parade"

description, but this is one case where a picture is worth a thousand words. The Irish Water Spaniel has to be seen—with its distinctive coat, composed of short curls, its deep liver color, its thin, tapering tail, almost devoid of hair, its typical topknot. The Irish Water Spaniel, by the way, has an undocked tail.

The breed is a development of two distinct strains found in Ireland prior to 1859, "The South Country Water Spaniel" and "The North Country Water Spaniel," with the former credited as the chief contributor in the perpetuation of the breed as we know it today. The breed is not generally fancied, but those who are familiar with the qualities of the dog have high praise for the "rat-tail." Percy K. Swan of Chico, California, as the foremost breeder of Irish Water Spaniels in this country, did much to promote the breed. Dogs which emanated from his kennels may be found in all parts of the land. Other enthusiasts, such as Dr. C. H. Searle of the Serlway Kennels at Franklin Park, Illinois, have joined Percy Swan in focusing attention on the Irish Water Spaniel's excellence as a water dog. He takes to water naturally and the quality of his coat, which is moisture shedding, is an important attribute, having gained the breed an enviable reputation as a duck retriever, but the coat has not been found so practical for upland game work, gathering burs, catching brush, tangling in briars, and so forth. Irish Water Spaniels are not so well known in the East as in the West and Middle West, though the patron club of the breed sponsored a Retriever trial in the East—at Montauk, New York, November 1940—intended to bring to the front the fine qualifications of the "rat-tail" dog. Chesapeakes, Labradors and Golden Retrievers dominated the various stakes—not a single Irish Water Spaniel was among the winners—nevertheless as a water dog, he is rated with the Chesapeake, Labrador, American Water Spaniel and the other Retriever breeds. In temperament he is not quick to make up with strangers, reluctant to do so in fact, and is at all times rather reserved in his manner. The Irish Water Spaniel, averaging 50 to 60 pounds, is plenty big for the job he is asked to do, but is no Hedy LaMarr for looks. He is unlikely to soar to the heights as a public favorite; however, his admirers are no less stanch because he is no conventional "beauty."

FLAT-COATED RETRIEVER

There have been sporadic bursts of attention to the Flat-Coated Retriever in this country, but no sustained interest in the breed, consequently since its introduction to the United States many years ago the Flat-Coated Retriever has never gained any degree of popularity or, indeed, mustered sufficient supporters to form a specialty club. As a consequence, sportsfolk on this continent have little

Flat-Coated Retriever

empirical knowledge concerning the working qualities of this dog, acknowledged in England to rank well up with the other Retriever breeds. There have been very few specimens seen in public, though Blackdale Ben of Wingan, a handsome individual, owned by Barbara Field Bliss, gained much favorable attention for the breed by the excellence of his performance in Retriever Trials during 1941.

The Flat-Coated Retriever may boast as pure a background as the other Retriever varieties, which is to say that there was some outcrossing and much interbreeding with dogs of similar type. The St. John's Newfoundland, probable forerunner of the modern Labrador Retriever, and the Labrador, too, are acknowledged to have played important roles in the development of the Flat-Coated Retriever. The latter is very much on the order of the Labrador—coat excepted, which is decidedly longer. Most specimens are wholly black in color, coat dense but of fine quality and texture, flat as possible, though the breed was formerly called wavy-coated.

A sturdily made dog of 60 to 70 pounds, the Flat-Coated Retriever is an efficient workman, a natural water dog, adept at marking, retrieving, and delivery, with style to please the most exacting. He has proved equally satisfactory for upland shooting as for waterfowl use. Just as he parallels the Labrador Retriever in many physical qualities, his temperament is somewhat similar too, and let it be added that the Flat-Coat is also a mighty close relative of the Golden Retriever.

CURLY-COATED RETRIEVER

This is certainly one of the oldest of all the recognized breeds now classified as Retrievers, the Curly-Coat popularly believed to be descended from the old English Water Spaniel. One glance at a representative specimen and it is easy to see how the Curly received its name, for it has a distinctive coat of crisp curls, somewhat similar to the Irish Water Spaniel, which probably figured as a cross in the ancestry. It is notable that solid liver is an accepted color of the Curly as well as the solid black.

While the exact origin of the Curly-Coated Retriever is a matter of conjecture, there is evidence to show that the Curly is a mixture of Water Spaniel, Retrieving Setter and the St. John's Newfoundland, plus a Poodle cross in the early 1880s. The Poodle was used in France as a retriever and it is believed this cross was undertaken to give the Curly its remarkable coat.

There is no question that the performance of the Curly rates well with the other Retrievers. In England at trials open to all Retriever breeds, the Curlies have demonstrated their ability to hold their own, with understandable variation in individual excellence just as is the case in other gun dog breeds. Some have greater dash and animation; fast, decisive; others are more deliberate in their work, plodding, but perhaps notable for getting results. While like the Flat-Coated Retriever, the Curly is more or less a rarity in the United States, it may be remarked that J. Gould Remick of Long

Island won his share of laurels with a pair of Curlies he showed in American Retriever Trials of a recent season. These dogs proved as proficient as leading representatives of other more popular breeds.

The Curly is noted for his stamina, his admirers boast of his tender mouth, and that the Curly is an exceptional dog in the water and his peculiar coat affords protection against the most punishing cover so that in a retrieving capacity on land the Curly is rated

Courtesy American Field, Chicago

Curly-Coated Retriever

excellent. Being affectionate, loyal, hardy, the Curly is said to be better gaited temperamentally to training than the other Retriever breeds, but it may be again stressed that the temperament variation is likely to be greater with individuals than as characteristic of different breeds.

AMERICAN WATER SPANIEL

The American Water Spaniel, or brown spaniel, as it was commonly called, has been familiar in the United States to upland bird hunters and wild-fowlers for many years. His effectiveness as a gunning companion endeared him to sportsmen, but because of the fact that he was never accorded breed recognition in an accredited stud book, the American Water Spaniel did not attain the popularity its abilities merited. However, in June of 1938 the Field Dog Stud Book, after exhaustive investigation of bloodlines and individuals for several generations, accepted the American Water Spaniel as pure-bred, and since that time other stud books have followed the FDSB leadership.

The dog is distinctively American, perhaps even more so than the Chesapeake Bay Dog. There is unverified romance in the legend about Columbus bringing over the first pair, but certainly 35 and 40 years ago this spaniel was the dog that accompanied many a youthful hunter on his early trips afield.

There is little reason to doubt that the Irish Water Spaniel, English Water Spaniel, and various other similar breeds contributed to the development of the American Brown Water Spaniel. Today the latter has true breed characteristics, exceptional intelligence, possesses extraordinary hunting propensities, courage, stamina, and aquatic abilities of a high order. The dog is favored as an all-around shooting dog, at home afield or astream. This breed works on land in spaniel fashion, depending on body scent for game location. They do not point game, but spring their quarry. The tail, always in motion, is nevertheless an unmistakable signal when game is scented. As a retriever, the American Water Spaniel marks well, gives ready and intelligent response to its handler, and game is brought in with dispatch and tender carry.

In the standard approved by the Field Dog Stud Book of Chicago, Illinois, the general appearance of the breed is described:

Medium in size, rather short in the legs, sturdy, typical spaniel character, curly coat or marcel effect, an active, muscular dog with emphasis placed on proper size and conformation, correct head properties, texture of coat, and color. Of amiable disposition, demeanor indicates intelligence, strength and endurance.

The color should be solid liver or dark chocolate, little white on toes and chest permissible. The height, 15 to 18 inches at the shoulder and range of weight from 25 to 45 pounds.

CHAPTER VI

Picking the Prospect

It is hoped that the brief historical background of each breed, its description and a little about the capabilities of the dog may prove helpful to the reader in deciding on the breed he wants to own. It should be stressed again that temperament in individual dogs varies greatly.

But let us suppose that you have picked out the breed you prefer. You now would like to have a little help in determining how to select a good specimen, one that has the latent qualities to develop into a useful hunting dog. Perhaps you have heard your "doggy" friends speak of the "choice puppy" of a litter, a favorite expression with many, but when a person has to do his choosing while the puppies are still very young, how in the world can one know which is the "choice" puppy?

The author has seen and examined thousands of litters of sporting dogs. He has looked puppies over carefully at all ages, from the time their eyes were closed tightly until precocious youngsters were ready for their initial romps in the field. Watching puppies develop, then witnessing their progress as they gained experience over a span of several years may prompt one to try to discern certain qualities in even the youngest prospect, but there is no infallible method of picking the best of the lot.

Because some of us, no matter how undeserved, get reputations as "experts," we are called upon to say which one in a particular litter is likely to be the "flier." Not to disappoint by a noncommittal answer, it is a general practice to indicate a specific puppy, then proceed to explain glibly why that youngster has the "makings" of a good one! This is largely the bunk. To be perfectly honest, it is

pure guesswork and all such predictions are fraught with uncer-
tainty. True, the experienced breeder can recognize particular
qualities that he believes will develop along proper lines, especially

A litter of Pointer puppies

if he is completely familiar with the genealogical background of the
litter, but to say without reservation that one puppy is going to be
the choice of the litter is mostly pure buncombe—or clairvoyance!

Litter of English Setter puppies

We are willing to concede, however, that the veteran dog man
seems able intuitively to pick the better prospects. Something about
a youngster, the air with which he carries himself, the look in his

eyes, certain puppy mannerisms—yet the most experienced cannot define precisely the qualities even though recognizing them at once.

There are precocious puppies, just like child prodigies. But until one has an opportunity to appraise the natural qualities, he simply

What goes on? Pointer puppy

is in the dark about real potentialities. It has always seemed to us that the veteran professional bird dog trainer and handler, Jake Bishop, summed it up wisely when he said:

"I never really know what I have until I have broken a dog. Some of the world-beaters fold up badly, others have the char-

Precocious English Setter puppies

acter and courage to come through the training routine and retain the fire, independence, and boldness we all like; but until the training process is complete, I never do much guessing as to how good one of my dogs is going to be."

What may be listed as prime considerations in the acquisition of a puppy are: (a) *Reliability* of the seller; (b) *Fashionability* of the puppy's breeding—how good are his bloodlines—and (c) *Individuality* of the puppy itself.

The suggestion is again advanced that the novice have an experienced "dog man" along when selecting a puppy. If this is not practical, one may safely take the word of a reputable breeder. Be

Pointer—Style, character, and intensity at 3 months!

sure that the youngster is pure-bred, that proper papers are available so that *your* dog may be registered in an authentic stud book, and find out what steps, if any, have been taken to immunize the puppy against distemper.

In reference to registration of your hunting dog, it might be interpolated that the *Field Dog Stud Book,* authentic all-breed registry,

A pair of three-month-old Pointers

published by the AMERICAN FIELD, Chicago, Illinois, records the greatest number of hunting dogs and this bureau affords records of remarkable accuracy and permanence.

You have, of course, decided to own a pointing dog—or a spaniel —or a Retriever. When you have chosen the breed, make it a point to learn something of the pedigrees of the outstanding dogs of that breed or at least consult with some one who is an authority on such breeding. Without good bloodlines, individual prowess may be an accident. If the dog you select is fashionably bred—that is to say, has a good ancestry with desirable lines combined—you can reasonably expect that he will prove worthy of your best training efforts. Does training received by the parents or other ancestors of a dog become a part of the puppy's heritage? There is little evidence

Pointer—3 months old

to support such a belief, but in the matter of temperament and character—well, that is something else again, for the dog may be better disposed to accept training.

The ambitious amateur trainer is urged to get a prospect of good pedigree because to the practical fancier this means that certain

Pointer pups get an early start in life

desirable characters are fixed in a family. You can depend on your youngster possessing the essential natural qualities if he comes from a strain bred judiciously for many generations with the family characters always conspicuous in the offspring. The value of the pedigree—and do not regard it merely as a compilation or conglomeration of names—lies in the fact that it represents continuous and careful selection of individuals and bloodlines to produce uniformity of type and elevate excellence of performance. A pedigree to some, like a treaty with the Axis powers, might be just another "scrap of paper," but to the practical breeder it is of undeniable value. Consult, if possible, an authority on the genealogy of the breed you fancy, for study and experience are necessary for proper evaluation of animal ancestry.

While there is considerable guess when it comes to picking out the best dog in a litter, nevertheless you can select the one that appeals to *you* most of all. Just keep in mind not to choose a puppy that is timid, shy, or physically unsound. Do not condemn a young-

Pointer puppy: Note cocked foreleg. Tail angle will likely improve

ster as timid just because he does not dash to you readily; dogs react differently to various stimuli and it is not always the exuberant youngster which will prove the best performer, though signs of eagerness do make an impression.

The usual expedients resorted to in an endeavor to determine which puppy might have the best potential nose—such as hiding a piece of meat, or setting a pan of milk out of sight of the pups—may be disregarded. And it really doesn't mean anything, as some may insist, that if you remove all of the litter from their sleeping box, the dam will pick up the best puppy first and carry it back to the bed.

Col. A. A. Thomas of Dayton, Ohio, had the best formula for choosing the puppy most likely to succeed. "If you want to determine which is the best puppy in a litter," said Colonel Thomas, "put them all in a yard surrounded by a fence a few feet high. The probabilities are that at first all of them will howl and try to get out. Some will give up after a few attempts, curl up and go to sleep, play among themselves or sit down and wistfully survey the fence; others will continue the attempts at scaling the walls for some time, but will evenutually give up and retire until only one puppy remains, and if he continues his efforts despite all failures until he succeeds in securing his liberty, take him; *he is the one you want.*" Determination is always a most valuable characteristic.

Do not buy a puppy less than two months of age, preferably ten weeks as a minimum, and not that young if a long train trip is to follow.

Early manifestation of pointing instinct

Just now we started to refer again to the importance of natural qualities and the thought came all unbidden that perhaps at this point many readers would be wondering about physical appearance. As in the case of horses, it can be said that hunting dogs run in all shapes and sizes. In every one of the sporting breeds, you will find many useful dogs that certainly do not approach bench show standards of excellence, yet in the field they are more than a match for dogs that have acquired sufficient points for a bench championship. Breeders of gun dogs, taken by and large, pay very little attention to conformation "bench points," though all are alert to see that the dog is physically equipped to do all that is expected of him. The average hunter who is likely to own just a dog or two and gun over him for several seasons, should not sacrifice more important qualities for mere appearance, but at the same time it is well for him to keep in mind that he might just as well select a dog easy to look at, one that he can proudly display to his friends when the hunting season is far off.

In the puppy, try to choose for good form and character. The former implies what will develop into the best proportioned frame and indicate stamina; by character is meant courage, ambition, intelligence. Some so-called authorities have recommended selection of the largest puppy in a litter, presumably on the ground that size is an indication of health and a strong constitution and endurance. But size can be detrimental in a field dog, especially when there is a

Inherent pointing tendencies

tendency to large frames or lumber in the strain. Conversely, don't pick "the runt" thinking you will confound your shooting companions when you prove just how good he is after development. Get a dog that has the physical qualifications of the breed to do his job proficiently and is possessed of attractive appearance.

Get a dog you are attracted to, a dog that seems to you to have personality, for do not forget that you will shortly become greatly attached to him. Rudyard Kipling wrote from experience when he penned the immortal lines about giving your heart to a dog to tear. Even the sorriest kind of a dog is likely to get under our skin; that is why we emphasize the importance of exercising every care at the very start to be sure that you obtain one that is likely to be most satisfactory.

But let's hie on to this training subject. You've got your puppy now and are ready for the preliminaries.

CHAPTER VII

Important Preliminaries

The average sporting dog owner who aspires to train his dog is too eager to get into actual obedience lessons. About this time, he is not only ready to ask, "What is the best lesson for a puppy?" but wants to begin the process of breaking his dog. In our judgment, it is essential that the dog's interest in hunting be excited first of all and the initial work should be that best calculated to accomplish this. There are some trainers who prefer to school the youngster in obedience lessons, give him usual yard training, before going afield, but we hold to outings in actual game environments as the proper way to get the sporting dog started. You *develop* and *train* hunting dogs, not simply exact obedience. Obedience is the basis of all training, but of greater importance is development, which means solely to give the dog's natural qualifications a chance to flower.

What is it you want to do? First, get a line on the dog's natural qualities and his particular temperament. Remember that his mission in life is to hunt for and find game; the goal is not merely an obedient dog, a mannerly one that performs perfectly, but mechanically. The trainer should always keep uppermost in mind that while it is possible to get practically irreproachable response in the way of obedience from a dog, this many times will not mean a thing when it comes to finding game in the field. More frequently than not, the mechanical performer which knows all the commands has his attention riveted on his handler, keeping ever alert to respond instantly to signals, when the dog's chief efforts should be directed toward finding game, his primary function. Concentrate on the fact that your purpose is to develop the dog's natural instincts, his desire to range, to hunt for and to locate game, and we believe that the

59

best way this can be done is to give the dog freedom of the field, allow him to get out and run, to flush and chase birds, to have a good time pursuing his hereditary predispositions, and thus gain knowledge of practical hunting. Don't hamper him with human restrictions or orders that tend to take away some of the zest; let him have a few of these outings without in any way endeavoring to exact obedience from him. Do not be idle, however; this is the chance on which you must capitalize—to study your dog, analyze his character, his peculiar temperament, estimate his potentialities. You can be busy determining his strong and weak points, noting the excellence of his nose, his boldness, or lack of it, and giving special heed to certain traits that should be given particular attention later. After a careful estimate of his qualities, you should clarify the "ideal" you have in mind, decide the kind of dog into which you intend to develop him, and then plan your training campaign fully before you begin any set lessons.

It goes without saying that all the answers to your training problems will not be found in this book. To be a successful trainer and develop brilliant performers, you have to possess a genius for solving the difficult situations with which you may at times be confronted. No author can hope to anticipate all of the trials and tribulations that prove so disconcerting to the amateur trainer, but there is no earthly reason why with patience and persistence even the veriest tyro cannot get good results by adapting what may be set forth in this system to the individual case. Never become discouraged. Your canine pupil may be coming along like a world-beater one day, and seem especially dull, even willful and perverse, the very next. Don't give up. It is a general rule that the dogs which require the most time and effort in training eventually become the best performers.

But we have wandered from our main theme of giving the dog some outings in the field before starting on your set course of yard training. Naturally, you will have taught your prospect a few elementary things, such as his name, the meaning of a common command, like "No," and undoubtedly to lead. It is not necessary to go beyond this. Very frequently in the case of an extremely young prospect, we have in the course of conversation remarked that the particular dog must teach himself to run. From the expressions on the faces of various listeners, we know that occasionally the remark has been grossly misunderstood. After seeing a dog dash madly along a roadway, they concluded that with such a great burst of speed as that displayed, there wasn't much about running the dog did not already know. But our comment was meant to connote more than mere fleetness of foot. Veteran trainers realize just what is meant. It is a short way of saying that the young dog should be given several outings in the field so that he can become accustomed to running under various conditions, over different kinds of terrain, encountering diversified types of cover, handling himself properly in the actual environments of game, but transcending all this, give his natural instinctive qualities a chance to develop.

In the case of the potential field trial dog, the trainer must be extremely careful early in the dog's training about harsh measures to enforce obedience. Certainly if you have ambitions to groom your dog for field competitions, give him thorough opportunity to develop in his own instinctive way. Resolve now never to attempt to rush or hurry the breaking of your hunting dog. If the dog is intended for shooting purposes only, the obedience factor may be emphasized more than in the case of field trial prospects. In the latter, every effort must be exerted to develop the dog without loss of his inherent fire, independence, initiative, courage, determination, and boldness.

Regardless of whether the dog is to be used exclusively as a shooting companion or developed as a field trial prospect, give him outings in the field before the complete yard training routine. Enlargement of hunting instinct is the principal objective; refinements of training, based on obedience, can always be attended to later, but unless the dog's natural bent for searching out game is encouraged and developed, it is unlikely that he will reach the heights which otherwise might be gained.

How old is the dog you intend to train? We do not recommend puppies younger than eight months, preferably a year of age. And if the dog is older, all the better, for he will have absorbed much that very likely shall prove useful to you in his quick development. Many successful field trial handlers take five and six month old bird dogs to the big open Canadian prairies and allow them to romp to their heart's content. But no effort is made to break these youngsters. They are just being permitted to find out for themselves what certain things are all about. Later on, when they are better able to absorb the lessons, the serious business of training commences.

There are precocious puppies which point at eight and ten weeks of age—mighty cute, too—but don't bank on these juvenile phenoms. True, some of these puppies may have the pointing instinct strongly ingrained; indeed, the reader undoubtedly has had the experience of one of his friends telling about his ten-month-old hunting dog over which he shot birds last open season. "He was as stanch as a

This puppy is pointing stanchly at an early age. Later in life, breaking tendencies will appear and regular training routine be indicated to steady the dog

five-year-old," the friend is almost sure to say, "and he came by it all naturally."

It is very true that the ten-month-old puppy pointed birds, held stanchly and was steady under the gun. But the very next season, if you asked that friend, the self-same puppy, "which broke himself," has discovered it is fun to rush in and disturb the birds, consequently he is very likely to be running wild, flushing his game, and chasing recklessly. But if he is now taken in hand and trained properly, an effective system followed, the lessons will not be soon forgotten. Many times an owner who shot over his ten-month-old setter or pointer, later sends the dog to a professional handler for additional training, and if the cycle described happens to come to pass at the period, the inexperienced owner is prone to criticize the professional trainer for undoing the fine *breaking* the owner had done while the dog was still a pup!

While we caution against attempting to handle very young puppies when giving them preliminary outings, do not deny yourself the pleasure of working with puppies, which is most interesting and when one can keep in daily touch with them and see them advance in their work, it affords much satisfaction and enjoyment. Puppies are just like children. We like to see them grow and develop, providing they progress along the right lines. Seek independence and natural quality in puppies. Do not endeavor at once to make the puppy "biddable." Many owners want a puppy which they can definitely control, one which will readily take on acquired qualities, and such a youngster ofttimes, in place of being independent, becomes dependent upon his handler to the extent that he becomes a mere automaton (independence and natural qualities being relegated to the discard). And thus what might have been a good prospect is frequently ruined! We do not mean to say that all puppies so handled turn out this way, but enough of them do so that it greatly reduces the number that carry on and make good All-Age dogs.

No man, let alone a dog, can do two things perfectly at one time. A dog cannot have his mind on birds and be hunting for them with fire, eagerness, and intensity, if, at the same time, he is constantly looking for orders from his handler.

In the case of Retrievers, it is the usual thing to see puppies, barely able to waddle, follow almost any tossed object, pick it up and start back as though to retrieve to hand. This is seemingly instinctive with them, and the trainer's function is merely highest development of the natural qualities possessed by the pupil.

But whether your prospect is of the pointing breeds, a spaniel, or a Retriever, you will early want to teach him his name. Napoleon made a classic remark that an army marches on its stomach, and we presume to paraphrase that to "the best way to teach a puppy its name is through its tummy." Do not conclude from this that a dog can be trained through his stomach. Or that an effective system can be builded solely around reward and punishment. But it is an easy way to familiarize the young puppy with its name by pronouncing it when you call him to you and reward him with a choice morsel. Decide on a distinctive name, one with an easily distinguished sound, preferably a single syllable, for authorities are not all agreed that dogs actually understand the words, many contending that the inflection of the voice or the intonation is what gets the response.

Any puppy will come cheerfully when you proffer a bit of food. Assume a squatting position or merely bend over, say only the dog's name and he will come to you cheerfully, willingly, promptly. When this has been repeated a few times you will be gratified to see how quickly the youngster has learned the name you have given him. Use the name whenever the opportunity affords. Do not at the outset add any other words of caution or command. When the routine of force training is commenced later on, a check cord can be used if necessary to supplement these kindergarten preliminaries. Subsequently, when you are teaching your prospect to sit or stand or remain kenneled up, you will be able to call other names and the particular dog will not respond until you say his own name. The person with several dogs in a single kennel pen will find this a useful method when he wants to have only one dog come out of the pen You can have several dogs sitting alertly, perhaps each eager to come, but none will move until the proper name is spoken, even though the dog right next to them may be called and respond.

In the case of large kennels, many keepers resort to the practice of tying up the individual dogs at feeding time. Short cords or chains are attached to their collars and the pan of food placed just in front. It is good practice to call out the name of the particular dog when preparing to feed him, and the novice often is astonished to observe how quickly each becomes familiar with his own name.

Perhaps the next simple command is "Come" or "Come here." This can be associated with the dog's name when calling the puppy to be fed. The importance of food in such training routine is considerable, though "rewards" should not be given too lavishly. Homing pigeons, incidentally, get their start with food as the attraction, and pigeoneers use feeding time for a test of their birds.

We might interpolate at this point that it is not our intention to give the exact set of commands the trainer must use. Certain words or phrases are preferred by individual handlers, and frequently we shall suggest as many as three or four commands for the same action, from which the reader may take his choice. But it should be stressed that you pick the particular word of command you are going to use

Photo by W. Eugene Smith

A fair Diana poses with a pair of Springer Spaniels, a Pointer, an English Setter, a Golden Labrador Retriever, a Golden Retriever and a Black Labrador Retriever

and stick to it. This will simplify education of your dog. A single command should be adopted for each act that a dog is required to perform, and that particular order should be used exclusively for that act. Don't confuse the dog, don't make it more difficult for him to comprehend by using a series of commands—"Down," "Charge," "Lie down," "Drop," each order for the same act. Decide on one command, preferably a single word, the shorter and more distinctive the sound, the better, and stick to it. The dog will learn more rapidly and his response will be consistent.

You can add certain words to your puppy's knowledge by making use of opportunities that will be frequently afforded. You will want him to understand "No," "Shame," and perhaps "Leave it," intended for things that he should not do or should desist from doing. If you cannot anticipate the dog's action, at least be alert that at the instant he does something he should not do, to voice the command, "No." Or in such instances you may prefer "Shame." In any event, be sure that the dog associates the admonition with what he should not have done. The same method is applied to "Leave it." When the puppy is indulging in some action that you do not approve, say to him "Leave it." The tone in which this order may be given is generally sufficient to get the desired results. During the early lessons, always use your normal talking voice, giving commands naturally, and no matter the provocation, do not raise your tones or commence "hollering." Excited shouting of instructions to a going dog is ordinarily not nearly so effective as calm, confident, natural voicing of orders, the tone friendly but firm.

CHAPTER VIII

Implements of Training

"I have six able serving men;
They taught me all I knew
Their names are *What* and *Where* and *When*
—and *How* and *Why* and *Who*."
—KIPLING

At this juncture it may be proper to mention the equipment that you will require for the training lessons—instruments to help you. Proper tools are essential for any purpose, and this applies to dog training. First of all, get a leather collar, a plain flat one, with ring to which a leather leash, four or five feet in length but strong, can be readily attached with snap and swivel. You will need both collar and leash when you teach your youngster to lead. This is something that may be done early in the puppy's life. You must also procure a "check cord;" a piece of light weight rope five yards in length is sufficient for yard training, but a longer rope may be required for use in the hunting field. Provide yourself with a dog whistle, metal or bakelite, the type with the "pea" or cork ball inside, on which different tones can be sounded. Practice blowing the whistle distinctively, but do not attempt to get and use a whistle entirely different from the standard kind of "dog whistle." We do not recommend the high-pitched, so-called "silent" whistle. While a dog is said to be able to hear vibrations up to 75,000 per second, the human ear attuned to a mere maximum of 13,000, nevertheless a trainer is wise to stick to the regular whistle. An Acme Thunderer is very satisfactory.

With equipment listed above, you will be ready to start yard work. But other implements of training are required as the education of your dog advances, particularly when you come to the lessons on force retrieving. You will then need a stripped corn-cob (the kernels removed), a sawbuck or retrieving dumbbell, a pistol, a whip, spike collar, and a small piece of wood, preferably oval in shape, about the

67

size of a turkey egg, covered with nails, the points of which project so that headless tacks or nails are desirable. A sawbuck, by the way, is nothing more than a small round stick—a portion about eight inches long of a broom handle can be used—with crossed pegs or X-shaped supports nailed to each end so that the dummy will rest on these legs no matter how it is put down or thrown. The purpose of the dumbbell, or the sawbuck, is to keep the cylindrical portion

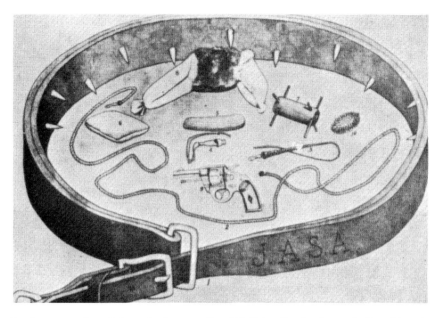

Implements of training: 1. force collar J.A.S.A., 2. check cord, 3. whip, 4. whistle, 5. corn cob, 6. cushion pad, 7. sawbuck, 8. dummy hare, 9. pistol, 10. wooden egg covered with shoemaker's heel nails

off the ground and make it easy for the dog to pick up the object.

For ages the whip has been regarded as an essential implement of dog training, although some authorities have relegated the whip to the discard and certain authors caution amateur trainers to shun the whip as they would the plague. These will tell you that punishment has no place in the training of a dog. This is another of those generalizations that simply do not prove applicable in all cases. It depends on the dog. You remember, "Spare the rod and spoil the child." This would not apply to every little boy and girl. But punishment intelligently meted out gets salutary results at

times in the education of many dogs. It is well to remember, however, that kindness pays the biggest dividends. Honey, let it be
said, still catches more flies than vinegar, and a dog actually gives
his best performance out of a desire to please his master, rather
than because of dread of the lash. You get such a greater thrill
from seeing a dog happily accomplish his work because he is doing
it to please, than one that goes fearfully about the task, cringing
perhaps because of fear of chastisement if a mistake is made.

Punishment should never be administered unless the dog can
readily associate it with a particular infraction; he should know
why he is being punished. Ordinarily, a mild reprimand will suffice,
an expression of disapproval of the dog's actions; if this isn't enough,
other means must be resorted to.

The whip, just as the spike collar, has its place in the training
regimen. Ask any veteran successful handler. Granted that there are
those who do not know how to use the whip properly, and it is even
conceded that the less one has to do with the whip the better in
many cases, nevertheless the whip can serve the trainer with occasional benefit. Its proper application demands perfect control of the
temper; punishment with the whip must be given at the exact psychological moment. Its use should be governed so that dogs do not
display fear at the very sight of it. Injudiciously used, dogs may
quickly discover that they can escape the punishment inflicted by
a whip by racing away, and even the veriest tyro of dog handler
is not long in finding out that it is better and easier to prevent faults
than correct them once they are acquired.

The whip should have a snap at the end which will make it easy
to tie on to your belt. The majority of professional handlers equip
themselves with quite a sturdy riding whip, composed of several
stiff pieces of leather sewed together, a bit flexible at the end, with
a leather loop at the top so that the whip can be slipped over the
wrist. There is generally a snap attached to the top leather loop.
The whip, although condemned by many, if properly used is very
effective in persuading a dog to remember his manners.

The spike collar has as many, if not more, critics than the whip.
But when intelligently and judiciously applied, it is considerably
more humane than other means of imparting the same degree of
knowledge to the dog. The spike collar, albeit a cruel looking instru-
ment to the uninitiated, is really less formidable than the ordinary

choke collar, which can come close to strangling a dog, whereas the spike arrangement is devised to get obedient action without danger of injury to the dog. Most readers of this book realize that the dog's "hide" is toughest around the neck. There are several designs of spike collars, all of which may be effectively used, though we prefer the J.A.S.A. Force Collar, manufactured and distributed by William E. Hulan, Hulan Leather Co., Shelbyville, Tenn.

This spike collar was designed and originally produced by our good friend, Señor J. A. Sanchez Antuñano of Merida, Yucatan, Mexico, an outstanding authority on the development and training of pointing dogs. The J.A.S.A. Force Collar is made of two pieces. The strap with the spikes is twenty inches long, one and one-half inches wide, with a ring at one end to assure easy sliding. The other piece of leather is for a ring and buckle, and for attaching the check cord. The short strap is two and a half inches long, one inch in width. The dimensions given are for a setter or pointer weighing in the neighborhood of fifty pounds, but the collar can be regulated to fit a cocker spaniel, or a larger size may be obtained through the distributor mentioned before.

The J.A.S.A. Force Collar has two rows of spikes, six on each side, with points which project three-eighths of an inch from the leather. As its designer claims for it, "this collar has the advantage over other kinds that the spikes are of necessary length to have effect only on the dog's hide without causing any internal injury, and it can be used with full confidence.

"To get the best results with use of the J.A.S.A. Force Collar," Señor Sanchez Antuñano explains, "when the trainer handles the dog at his right side (dog's left side), or with his right hand, the collar should be as shown in the illustration, figures 2 and 3. When the trainer is left-handed, or handles the dog with his left hand, the collar should be used as shown in figure 1, otherwise the collar won't tighten or loosen up the moment desired."

The pistol of course is used to accustom the dog to the report of firearms and the other implements depicted have equally obvious uses or will be explained at some length in subsequent chapters. Of course, the ambitious handler may devise other objects to assist him in his retrieving lessons; for example, a piece of stiff rubber hose can be substituted for a corncob.

At this point the reader is again reminded that punishment in training a hunting dog is administered chiefly as a means of correcting misdemeanors and imparting knowledge of what is right and wrong. It is of utmost importance that the act and the punishment are so closely connected that the dog associates one with the other. The whip, check cord, force collar, and other instruments of chastisement or restraint are held to be essential to good breaking of the hunting dog, but they must be used intelligently. Some dogs can be trained without the need of any harsh measures; there are

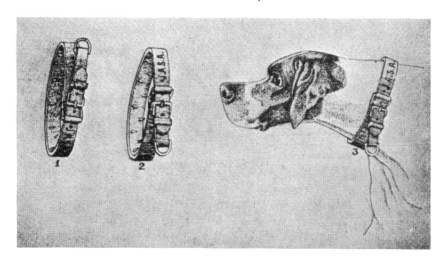

Manner of using the J.A.S.A. force collar

others where these implements are of undeniable aid and benefit in the education of the dog.

The educator is urged to be careful in the application of force and also cautious about extending extravagant praise. A woman's intuition is far from being so highly developed as a dog's keenness for judging different people. Is it telepathy? However it is transmitted, the dog seems able to perceive the mood of a person, and especially one engaged in training him. The breaker should never undertake to teach his dog anything when in an angry mood; you can't let your temper run away and be a success at developing a good hunting dog. You simply cannot afford to try to conceal your true feelings from the dog; his reactions are likely to be in accord with your emotions. Be sure to have a feeling of genuine friendliness for your canine pupil. And don't do things in a way that will confuse or annoy him. Take for example the way some people pet a dog. You can't just grab at the dog—he may pull away thinking your gesture is an attempt to strike him—nor is it soothing to his nerves to be patted sharply, like an impatient caller rapping on a door. Around high strung dogs particularly, it is important to be calm, not jerky or erratic in movements, skillfully soothing. Incidentally, stroke a dog by laying the hand on the dog slowly, palm flat against his body, the whole hand caressing him gently and with long strokes, and the voice should be equally soft and reassuring.

CHAPTER IX

Early Lessons

Sporting dogs do not have to be coddled. You will find that the individuals of the popular sporting breeds have the character and courage to face the stern realities of life. The majority of practical hunting dogs are housed in kennels, but just in case the reader may want to keep his canine hunting pal in the house, something about housebreaking will be included here. However, it isn't necessary to make a "spoiled" pet of your dog. We do recommend that you get on intimate terms, become his pal and hunting partner and make of him a most delightful companion. The sporting dog has character, self-respect, consequently does not like to be constantly fawned upon. Not that "man's best friend" doesn't want to be on the most amicable basis with his master, but undue sentimentalism is not called for; the well bred sporting dog, while actually tolerating the fawning ministrations of an overzealous master or mistress, looks on this as "kid stuff." A close companionship and unswerving loyalty can be maintained on just as sound if a less demonstrative basis. This, of course, varies with different dogs, but it is ordinarily sufficient if you let your dog know when he pleases you, make him understand that he is appreciated, but do not disturb him with continual outbursts of affectionate friendliness and sentimental regard. We realize that some of these remarks are entirely uncalled for in a book of this nature, where the reader is more or less a sophisticated "dog man," but for the benefit of the few we want to speak in behalf of the dog being permitted to lead a normal "private" life!

The act of housebreaking your puppy, training him to live in the house, can be accomplished easily, naturally. It is a comparatively simple job and since it will obviate cleaning up every morning a disagreeable mess where the puppy has dropped his "calling card" in answer to nature's summons, you are expected to tackle the task at once if you intend to keep the youngster indoors most of the time.

Observation of the puppy's natural habits is the first requirement. The youngster will desire relief several times in the course of the day, generally shortly after awakening from a nap and also soon after each meal. There will be other occasions, such as subsequent to a session of play, when he may "forget." But you can forestall this. If you watch him carefully you will perceive telltale signs. He will show by his actions that he is seeking a place to relieve himself; he will become restive and very likely run around and around, sniffing here and there. This is your cue. Pick him up immediately by the back of the neck and carry him outdoors. Just as soon as he has relieved the urge, allow him to return indoors. He will get to understand what is required very quickly and once the puppy accepts the routine, you can count on it becoming habitual. He will give unmistakable signs to you thereafter.

Rarely will the average healthy youngster soil the place where he sleeps and once the puppy is old enough to realize the niceties, he can be restrained to his sleeping quarters where he learns to postpone ordinary impulses until he can find a place other than in immediate proximity to his sleeping box. If the puppy makes a mistake, it is sufficient to take the culprit to the spot where the offense occurred, reprove him by scolding him, and add a gentle shake or two. Some suggest that you rub his nose in the uncleanliness as a corrective measure, but this is not really necessary. Merely scrub the spot with a sufficiently strong solution—creoline or advertised preparation—to make the area unattractive because of its disagreeable smell. Regularity is what gets results. Feed the puppy on a definite schedule, give him outings spaced about two or three hours apart, encourage regularity in his habits.

When you take the youngster outside and he finds a place for relief, on the next occasion take him to the same vicinity. The dog likes to use the same location or one that has been visited by other canines. When you find the places which hold a special attraction, you can make the rounds and the dog by this time will have come to understand the principal purpose of the routine. Once the puppy has done his job, take him indoors again. Do not permit use

Photo by W. Eugene Smith

A restful interlude as trainer looks down at a group of hunting dogs having a respite on a warm day

of a place that may prove annoying to your neighbor or the public at large.

Newspapers on the floor as a depository for excretions? No. Some visitor may step in the purge and with children around this system is especially objectionable. The best method is to take the puppy out of doors at regular intervals and in a very short while you will be gratified to have the youngster indicating when the housebroken requirements of nature demand a "relief expedition." In case an old housebroken dog slips, he should be disciplined at once, and if he persists after the first reprimand, it may be necessary to "confine him to quarters" for a day or two.

Introducing your sporting dog puppy to the collar and lead will be among the first things for you to do. You can manage this when taking him to the field for his preliminary romps. From the immediate reaction of the youngster when the collar and leash is first felt, it may seem that this lesson is going to require some time, but actually the dog will quickly become accustomed to both the collar and the lead. The collar, a simple leather one with a ring to which the lead can be readily attached, should fit snugly enough to prevent being pulled off over the dog's head, yet it must not be so tight as to choke the dog. When the collar with lead attached is slipped on for the first time, the puppy will not hesitate to give notice that he doesn't fancy this new restraint. More likely than not, he'll begin cutting up like a couple of rug-cutters at a Harlem ball, jumping, whirling, bucking and bounding, a canine Dervish, and his efforts to free himself may be at once awkward and ludicrous. It is up to you to see that his struggles are ineffective, unavailing. Just keep a stout hold on the lead. It really won't be long until the youngster wears himself down, decides he might as well submit and docilely comes alongside of you. Stroke him in your most friendly manner and start to walk. This may prove the fuse to set off another display of temper, but it will not long endure and in a very few minutes you'll be able to lead him wherever you please.

But suppose, after a few jumps, the pup decides to sulk, drops to the ground and doesn't want to budge? Don't pull and haul! If you haven't somebody around who can prod him with a few light licks from behind, merely change to the force collar and the stubbornness will be quickly taken out of him. You can use the J.A.S.A. Force Collar like a simple leather one by reversing it, the spikes on the outside. If you are so using this collar, on an extremely obstreperous pupil, turn the spike side to contact his neck. The spikes are very effective "persuaders."

Once the puppy submits, make a display over him, regain his friendship and confidence, lead him around where it is quiet and there is nothing to distract him or frighten him, get chummy and then, after a short time, return him to his kennel. It is of importance to keep early lessons brief.

We want to emphasize at this point that all of the early lessons should be of short duration. The dog tires quickly and prolonged lessons can shorten the trainer's temper, too. Besides, you want the dog to be going through his routine enthusiastically, so aim to keep the lessons interesting to him. When you are teaching, be firm, exact prompt obedience and accurate compliance with commands, do not countenance slipshod performance, but once the lesson is at an end, let your dog enjoy himself in his own way—and have a little fun yourself watching his antics or playing with him. To paraphrase an old saw, all work and no play makes for a dull dog. Just as the manner in which you give commands should be clear, crisp, distinctive, the training lessons should be kept short, interesting, zestful. And select a quiet place, a suitable environment. Don't attempt the early lessons in a place with as many distractions as the Grand Central depot.

Your dog has been taught to lead properly, he has been permitted excursions in the field so that his hunting instincts are developing, and you have been able to appraise to an extent his potentialities. You are now ready to begin the yard training routine in earnest.

YARD TRAINING.—The elementary portion of yard training is already well under way when you have taught the dog his name, succeeded in having him come to you when called, when he responds to such simple orders as "kennel up," and has learned to lead. The dog is now ready for the lesson, HEEL. Then will come in order, SIT, and DOWN, that is, if you want your dog to drop. It is proper for a spaniel to sit; pointing dogs may drop, although stylists prefer to have setters and pointers remaining standing up. Sometimes particular bird dogs will have a tendency to drop under certain conditions, apparently an instinctive reaction, whereas in other cases the methods employed by trainers have the effect of causing a dog to go down. Do not require your pointer or setter to drop unless you have in mind a specific purpose for doing so.

Your dog is not considered finished with his yard training curriculum until he not only responds to spoken commands readily, but obeys the signals you may teach him without a single word being spoken. In this connection, many successful trainers use whistle signals rather than spoken commands or motions with the hands and arms.

TEACHING TO HEEL.—You proceed as in the lesson to lead, putting a collar on the dog with a suitable short leash. If this is your first attempt, better use a plain collar, but if you have had experience in the handling of dogs and are somewhat familiar with the tech-

Ready to begin the lesson in "heeling"

nique to be employed, you will get quicker and even more satis-factory results with the use of a J.A.S.A. Force Collar.

Most dogs are taught to heel at the left side of the trainer. This is solely a matter of personal preference. The practical gunner when training his dog will teach him to heel on the side opposite to that on which he generally carries his gun.

Give the command, "HEEL," and accompany it with a slight tap of your left hand against your left leg,—we are assuming that you will have the pupil on your left side. In case this is not true, simply substitute "right" for "left" in these instructions. You will have a fairly short hold on the leash with your left hand, the balance of the leather passed through to your right hand. Bring the dog up to your left side with his head parallel with your left knee and begin walking forward. Do not break into a trot nor do not proceed at too leisurely a pace. You want the dog to move along alertly. If the pupil displays a tendency to drop back, bring him up to the proper position with a light jerk accompanied by the order, "Heel." Be sure to exercise sufficient control with the lead so that the dog is not permitted to wander from your side. The canine student may seek to forge ahead of you, in which case he is at once returned to proper position with another light jerk, at which instant the command, "Heel," is repeated. At such times as the dog is heeling properly, you may take opportunity to encourage him with a word of praise and a friendly pat on the head, but do not overdo the praise or in any way confuse the dog. Repeat the order, "Heel," as you go along. In the event that the dog tries continually to get in front of you, you can supplement the jerk by tapping his nose lightly with the free end of the lead, or you can swing the loose end with your right hand, keeping it going like a pinwheel in front of you, and as this passes each time it will have the very effect you wish, that of discouraging his attempts to get out ahead and keeping the dog's head parallel with your left knee.

Do not countenance any half-hearted heeling on the part of the dog. Don't let his attention or his footsteps wander. Slipshod performance should never be accepted. Keep him in proper position at all times, have him alert. In the case of Retrievers their usefulness depends on the accuracy with which they are in position to mark the fall of game. This is one of the prime reasons for having the dog heel parallel with your left knee—not *behind* you—for it is also up to him to see what happens out ahead. In case the dog seems lackadaisical, you can keep his interest keen by holding a tidbit in your left hand and occasionally giving him a little of it.

After you have your pupil responding immediately to the command "Heel" and the signal, a tap on your left leg, this lesson has been mastered. You can teach the dog to follow properly at turns with simple additions to the routine described. With the canine pupil positioned properly and following at heel as you walk in a straight line, give the order, "Heel," and at the same time permit the lead to slide through your left hand, draw it tautly across the front of your body with the right hand. This will have the effect of bringing the dog around and of keeping him in heeling position at the turn. If the dog exhibits an inclination to cut across to your right side, flick him on the muzzle as you bring him into his correct position.

For the left turn, you step sharply to the left, bringing your right leg abruptly across in front of your left, so that your right knee serves as a barrier to the advance of the dog in the straight line you had been traveling. Give the command, "Heel," as described

Photo by W. Eugene Smith
A pair of Pointers "at heel"

before, have a firm hold on the check lead with your left hand and keep the dog in position as he makes the turn with you.

For an about-face or right-about turn, follow the method outlined for the right turn except that you will reverse your direction sharply, without a waste of steps, pivoting in your tracks as it were, like basketball players do. Give the order, use the lead in your right hand across the front of your body to bring the dog around with you, and proceed at once in the direction opposite to that in which you had been walking. Let us repeat, always walk briskly. Keep the dog keen. Don't be content with anything less than prompt, accurate, complete response to your commands.

When you are teaching your dog to heel, do everything crisply, with a businesslike air. Let the dog know this isn't fun, but serious business for him continuously; you should gaze straight ahead, walk at a good clip and you can tell without peering down at him whether or not he is in the correct position. Ignore entirely any minor nervous reaction on the part of the dog. Don't attempt to reassure him in case he appears frightened. He has to feel it is everyday stuff. If by chance the dog should pull from you and get on the opposite side of some obstacle, such as a tree or fence post, pause while he extricates himself from this difficulty, but do not back up to him. Stand still and let him get out of the situation and then be returned to your side.

As you perfect the dog's schooling in the art of heeling, you will be able to command his obedience with the spoken order or merely the sign without uttering a single word.

"SIT."—Here is another easy lesson and one that the novice trainer will enjoy giving, for one perceives the quick results. The tyro trainer feels a sort of genuine satisfaction because of the readiness with which he puts a dog in a sitting position and shortly receives obedience to the command. The first method to be described is simplicity itself. With the collar in place and the lead attached, stand facing the dog, take hold of the leather about eighteen inches above the dog's head, then as you give the order, "Sit," raise your left hand holding the lead to bring the dog's head up and at the same time lean over and with the full inside of your right hand press down on the rear part of the dog's back, or rump, thus forcing his hindquarters to a sitting position; by maintaining a firm hold on the leash you keep the dog's forelegs under him and his head raised. Repeat the lesson. After a few times, when you give the command, "Sit," it will not be necessary to place your right hand on the dog's back, but will prove sufficient if you just flick lightly with the loose end of the leash the hindquarters of the dog, for when he feels the touch he will assume a sitting posture. Very quickly, the order itself, with no more than an upraised index finger of the right hand as a signal, will be enough to get prompt obedience.

There is another simple way of teaching the dog to sit. You do not need either collar or lead. Face the dog and take hold of him under the chin, grasping a fold of skin on the neck. As you give the command, "Sit," pull the dog toward you slightly, then immediately and firmly push him back—and he will at once be forced into a sitting position. There is nothing to it at all. If you haven't already tried it, you will be astonished at the ease with which it is accom-

Pressure on lower part of back to place dog in sitting position

plished. As you pull the dog forward, he attempts to move toward you, is caught off balance by the sudden reversal of pressure and readily assumes a squat when you firmly shove back.

In the case of Retrievers, especially, and of spaniels to an extent, or even with setters and pointers, the trainer will want to teach the dog to sit in the heeling position. This is a natural follow-up to the lesson "Heel." It is accomplished in the manner described heretofore. The instructor halts suddenly, with the dog in the correct heeling position, then bends over the dog, places his left hand on the hindquarters and applies pressure to force the dog into the sitting position, while maintaining a taut lead with the right hand which

keeps the dog's head up and forelegs under him. The educator
should not change the position of his feet. When he resumes an
erect position, he should be facing the direction in which he had
been walking with the dog sitting at his left side. If the dog is
disposed to sit too far away, apply pressure to the side and back,
forcing him to assume the position correctly.

Steadiness in the sitting position requires special instruction. This

Photo by W. Eugene Smith
A Springer Spaniel is placed in the "Sit" or "Hup" position

will be dealt with at some length in the succeeding chapter, but first
it should be repeated that some breakers may not want their setters
and pointers to sit or drop. The preferred attitude for pointing dogs
is to stand motionless. To accomplish this, the command most generally used is "Whoa," although it was common in earlier days for
handlers to use "To-Ho" (pronounced Ter-ho), which has evolved
into "Whoa," a command used in the case of horses as well as
hunting dogs. It means stop, halt, stand still, remain motionless,
stay where you are. That's what you want the hunting dog to do
and the sound of order, "Whoa," is distinctive, and can be voiced
in tones that seem to compel immediate compliance.

CHAPTER X

Teaching the Dog to "Whoa!"

Teaching the pointer or setter to "Whoa," or the spaniel and Retriever to gain steadiness in the "Sit" or "Hup" position, can have the ground-work laid at feeding time. There are many able professional handlers of bird dogs who will tell you without reservation that *Whoa* should take precedence over all other commands. If you are able to stop your dog when you want and where you want, unquestionably you are in good position to exact obedience to other commands as well.

Select a quiet place, free from distractions. Place the dog's pan of food a little distance in front of him, say about four feet, and hold him away, while you voice the command, "Whoa," gently, firmly. Stroke him soothingly as you restrain him, but keep him standing motionless. At the outset, don't hold him for more than a few moments, then cheerfully order "Go on" and permit the dog to charge the feed pan. Repeat this lesson for several days, gradually increasing the length of time that you keep the dog waiting immobile and also extend the distance from his feed pan. You want to accustom the dog to the sound of the injunction, "Whoa," and to have him understand its implication. Subsequently, put on his collar and attach a check cord. The procedure is very much the same except that you permit the dog to start for the feeding utensil, then gently pull him up a certain distance from the food, holding the check line firmly. Release the pressure quite promptly and, giving the encouraging order, "Go on," let him continue the rest of the way. You will gradually lengthen the distance until you are stopping the dog quite a long way off from the pan. Later, when you have started him with the encouraging "Go on," but just before he reaches the pan, you will again enjoin him, "Whoa," and after repeating the lesson a few times, permit him to eat. Great patience must be exercised; don't try to hurry this portion of the dog's education.

You are now ready to teach the dog to "Whoa" whenever he hears the command. Elaborate rather than haphazard instructions get the best results. At first it may seem that you do not make much progress, but you very shortly should be able to compel obedience to the order, "Whoa," and stop the dog only a few feet from his feed pan. Now you proceed with the following lesson and it is one that will likely tax your patience.

Drive two sturdy stakes into the earth with about four feet of post above the ground. A distance of at least two rods should separate the posts. Tie a check cord of about fifteen feet to one stake and attach the other end to the force collar on your dog. Be precise in the measurement of the cord so that you know the exact spot to which it reaches and where it will halt your dog's forward progress. With a regular leather leash also attached to the collar, and with your dog at your side, commence walking away from the stake. Just at the instant you reach the end of the cord, command "Whoa," then take two smooth steps to the front and turn facing your dog, keeping the leash taut. Repeat the command and endeavor to keep the dog motionless. Caught between two anchors, as it were, he will likely begin to flounder about, or he may lie down. Be firm in your purpose. Force him to remain standing; you can help your dog to comprehend by standing perfectly still in front of him, braced to resist his movements. Voice the command, "Whoa," and keep the dog in position; when he moves, gently replace him where he originally stood. Try this lesson three or four times, then let your dog romp and play, for you do not want him to sour.

When you have succeeded in stopping him on command and he remains standing motionless, you can begin to move about, but only in front of him, keeping the dog in exactly the same position. Undoubtedly the dog will move. You must at once, this time more firmly, restore him to the original position. Just as you start again, more than likely he will move again. Replace him. No movement on the dog's part is too slight to go unnoticed or be ignored by you. It may mean continual repetition, but only by demanding the utmost accuracy in obeying the command can you hope for the fine success which should crown your persevering efforts.

Subsequently, you shall want to move to the sides and around the dog, but difficulties will arise at once, for the dog, you may be sure, will turn to face you in order to keep you in sight. This must not be permitted. With the dog checked at the end of the cord and quiescent, attach the leash to the second stake in front of the dog; this will help to keep him in a definite position. As you move deliberately to the side of the dog, bend over and have your hands so positioned that you can keep him standing "in line"; that is, your

Requiring steadiness in the "Sit" position. Trainer circles dog while canine pupil sits quietly

left hand should be at the side of his head to preclude his turning to watch you, and the right hand placed near the back of the dog on the right flank to prevent him moving his hindquarters in that direction; thus you have him under control. Don't wait for the dog to turn. You can gamble that he will do it, so be prepared in advance. It is worth repeating that it is much easier to anticipate a fault, prevent its happening, than it is to correct an error after it has been made.

When you have succeeded in keeping the dog standing and

facing forward while you move to his side, you may stand erect, but be alert to bend and stop his turning. Having reached this stage in the lesson, begin to walk around the dog, but if the dog does not stay absolutely still, you must utter the mandate, "Whoa," sharply, and at once replace him in position. You have your canine pupil sufficiently advanced to combine steadiness to this command with the lesson also teaching steadiness in the "sit" position. It is a good idea to alternate these lessons when you have come this far.

Photo by W. Eugene Smith

Labrador Retriever is steady in "sit" position. Note trainer's method of giving this signal

Exacting steadiness in the "sit" or "hup" position, the trainer places a force collar on the dog with a leash attached. The command, "Sit" is given, as explained in a previous chapter. With the dog in proper position, the instructor begins to walk around the pupil, repeating sibilantly, "Steady." As stated previously, the dog will want to turn and keep the breaker in view. You may anticipate this by uttering, "Sit, Steady," and checking the dog lightly. If he moves, replace him in the original position. Keep the leash up over his back so there will be no chance of tangling it. In this way a fairly taut line is maintained and you can readily check the dog. As you walk in a circle around him, keep repeating, "Steady," and do not overlook any movement on the part of the dog, no matter how slight. You can supplement the word of command with a hand sign and later a whistle signal. You gradually widen the circuit and when the dog has been perfected in the sit position, merely drop the leash on his back and proceed with the routine. The dog must not be allowed to move from the spot; return at once to replace him in case of the slightest movement. It should not be long until he understands fully and remains positively still.

A very similar procedure, with two cords of adequate length, is used to gain steadiness in the standing position to the order, "Whoa." You walk around the pupil as described, requiring absolute steadiness, after which you reach the point to inculcate obedience to the uplifted right arm sign and finally the whistle signal. Have the check cord tied to the post and attached to the collar as outlined earlier, with a long leash also held in your hand. Walk several yards in front of the dog, beyond the extent of the cord tied to the post, then call the dog to you, taking up the slack on the lead rope as the dog approaches. Get him to come on the run. Just as he reaches the end of the check cord, lift your right arm high over your head and while holding it vertical, voice the command, "Whoa." The dog is forced to halt by the cord attached to the post and the leash is tightened. It is imperative that you give the command and arm sign at precisely the instant he reaches the end of the cord, or just a split second before the impact in order to convey to the dog the wisdom of immediate obedience—or else! You hold the dog motionless by tension on both cords. Do not permit him to crouch or sit down. Should he do either, make him stand up at once; lift him by his hindquarters and after propping him up, return to your position prior to the interruption. After the dog has stood quite still for a brief period, go to him and express your gratification by words of praise plus some affectionate petting. You should have carefully avoided using any words other than the commands to guard against confusing the dog, but now you may feel free to praise him profusely for doing what you desired of him.

Repeat this lesson several times, but after each training session be sure to have a playful period afield with him, because breaking, no matter how skillfully handled, will tend to dampen the natural exuberance of the dog, and you want to have him retain his zest, enthusiasm, cheerfulness, high spirits, and initiative.

It is essential that you change the training territory frequently during the course of this lesson. And do not always use exactly the same distance from the post. You do not want the dog to associate any particular spot with the command, or any set distance; the intent is to make him understand the desirability of stopping at once when the order "Whoa" or the sign, right arm uplifted with palm facing dog, is given. Induce the dog to race away from the post in different directions. The faster he goes, the more quickly your goal will be attained. Being brought up with a jerk quickly persuades the dog to obey instantaneously your command and sign.

When after much repetition the dog halts at the spoken word or the signal, he may be permitted to go through the lesson loose. Have the collar and check cord attached—let the dog drag the cord —a precautionary measure. Should the dog at any time fail to stop when the command is given, return him to the precise spot where he was ordered to "Whoa," then withdraw to your previous position. Keep him standing there until he hears "Go on."

Persistency is the keynote of success. You may have to do it over and over again, but once you have succeeded in making your dog obedient to this command, you have achieved much in his education. Such celebrated professional handlers as George Payton, Dewey English, George Crangle, Ray Smith, Thomas Lunsford and a host of others consider "Whoa" of prime importance in the training of the gun dog. Indeed, George Payton has put sound training advice in the recommendation to owners that two commands are essential, "Whoa," and "Come Here," the latter to be discussed in the next chapter.

CHAPTER XI

Coming When Called

It may seem that this lesson is a repetition of one previously discussed. Even before any serious training was undertaken, you had taught your dog to respond to his name and had him coming to you when called. Perhaps you had induced prompt obedience by offering a choice tidbit. Or you may simply have said, "Come in," and slapped both of your hands against your knees, using only persuasive tones to coax the dog to recognize his master. You no doubt have discovered that crouching like a baseball catcher behind the home plate, or going down on one knee, encouraged immediate obedience on the part of the dog. Under the circumstances, you are not likely to encounter any real difficulties in having the pupil absorb this lesson of enforced response, but its place in the yard training curriculum is of importance because it convinces the dog that whether or not he wants to do so, he must come to you when called.

Attach the force collar and check cord. Command your dog, "Whoa," and then walk about ten or fifteen feet ahead of him. Turn and give the order, "Come in," adding the dog's name, if you wish. The instant the behest is uttered, jerk the cord sharply so that he will approach with alacrity. When he does, stroke him affectionately and use a few endearing terms.

Your intention is to have the dog come in to you at the instant he hears the command. Be careful not to check him with the cord and collar after he once starts in your direction. That might confuse him, for he would associate the punishment with coming in to the trainer. Never allow this to happen and never, under any circumstances, call a dog to you for punishment. Always go and get him or await his return, as may be expedient, but be sure that the dog clearly associates the punishment with the act of disobedience or the fault he committed.

If the dog lies down, merely check him into response, encouraging him once he has started in your direction. It may be that the dog will turn and start in a different direction. When he does this, be

Photo by W. Eugene Smith
Well-mannered troupe of Springer Spaniels with their trainer, M. J. Hogan

quick to take the opposite direction and check the dog severely. Never follow the same direction as that taken by the dog; under no conditions is he to assume the lead.

It should not take long for the dog to realize that he runs into punishment every time he attempts to dash away, and that only by running toward his handler does he escape it. When he comes to you, let the dog know by your affectionate greeting that he has done right. If by chance he does not approach as rapidly as you wish, it is a good idea to move backwards away from him, urging with "come along" or "hurry up" and this will result in acceleration of his pace.

After you have the dog coming in promptly and at good speed, be on the alert for a common sequel to this lesson. Most dogs, even after they understand what is desired, crave another test to determine whether or not they didn't give up too much of their rights when they obeyed readily. Be prepared, therefore, when your dog another day suddenly starts on a tangent. Don't shout or get excited. If anything, give the dog a little leeway, allow sufficient slack in the cord for him to get under way, and when his momentum has been stepped up, brace yourself as he reaches the end of the check cord and command sternly, "Come in," at the same instant yanking him severely, even causing a backward somersault. Immediately order again, "Come in," accompanied by another pull, and the odds are great that the dog will run quickly to you. The dog may even wag his tail gleefully, with an expression that says, "Well, it didn't work," and the trainer may feel a glow of satisfaction, because now the dog understands thoroughly that when he obeys readily, he is sure to escape punishment.

The dog may be permitted to drag the check cord freely in the field, but do not give the "Come in" order unless you are reasonably sure of the response of the dog or your ability to coerce him. If the dog and cord are out of reach when you utter the command, the dog may take advantage of the situation, and you will have a great deal of difficulty undoing that single training faux pas. If you allow the dog to drag the loose cord and want to order "Come in," be positively sure that in the event the canine does not obey at once, you can pick up the check cord and enforce immediate obe-dience.

In connection with this lesson, it is well to have the dog become familiar with whistle signals. Actually, hunting dogs more or less instinctively heed the whistle. A great deal of instruction is not necessary. But you can, after you have the dog sufficiently advanced to respond with alacrity to the command, "Come in," start to use the whistle. A distinctive note on the whistle, accompanied by a light check with the cord, will soon teach the dog the meaning of this signal. When the dog realizes that the whistle means for him to come in, the educator may also use the crack of a whip as a signal. This isn't necessary, but using the whip in such way induces a dog to come in to you, rather than to be inclined to shy off at sight of the whip. Of course, the dog may be frightened at the outset, but with recourse to the cord you bring him in, and when he has come to you lay the whip gently on his back. Don't crack it repeatedly; let the dog learn that the snap of the whip represents a signal for him to come in, and that when he responds promptly he is safe from harm. With application of proper methods the results of this routine will prove gratifying.

The proper introduction of the whip is of equal significance to introducing the firearm. None of us like to see a dog show fear and a tendency to slink off and run away at the sight of the whip. If the dog is taught that the whip can be harmless, he will not give the impression of some which cringe and start away to try to avoid it.

Speaking of the whistle, trainers of Retrievers and of spaniels will find it of invaluable assistance to have a special blast or shrill note which will have a similar effect to the spoken command, "Whoa." This whistle signal should be one that will stop the dog in his tracks. The dog may be schooled in his response by following the procedure outlined in the lesson on teaching the order, "Whoa." Make sure that this distinctive whistle signal is well understood. Its purpose is to stop the dog where he happens to be, principally for receiving orders, but such obedience will be found advantageous in a variety of situations. For instance, the person handling a Retriever may want to stop his dog in a particular place in order to give directions, or turn him at once from a short cast. Even in the case of a pointer or setter, such a whistle signal can prove beneficial. Suppose you are working a brace of dogs and one establishes a pretty point just under the brow of a hill. The game, a bevy of quail, say, is likely to be right at the crest. As you approach to flush, you notice the bracemate coming up on the far side of the slope, traveling downwind, and you immediately perceive that the pointing dog will not come into the bracemate's vision in time for a back at sight, and without favor of the wind undoubtedly the dog will flush the birds being pointed by the other. If you have a whistle signal that will cause the dog to halt in his tracks, you have saved the situation and everything can proceed in order and good shooting will be afforded, whereas if you were unable to warn or halt the dog any number of things might happen.

The use of the whistle and of an intelligent method of making the dog familiar with the whip and its utter harmlessness except when he deliberately does not respond as he has been *taught* to do, prepares the dog for his advanced field training. Outside of the ranks of professional handlers and a few leather-lunged amateurs, we cannot all go out into the field and shout orders to a hunting dog for several hours without developing a bad case of laryngitis, hence the importance of whistle signals and cutting spoken commands to a minimum. Under normal hunting conditions, the whistle is entirely satisfactory, though it must be said that in present-day field trial competition more and more professional handlers are coming to the use of their voice to direct their dogs, owing to the fact that if a dog is trained entirely to whistle signals, an opposing handler, even unwittingly, may simulate to an extent the tones of another's whistle and this would result perhaps in confusion for both dogs.

It isn't good practice to be shouting orders while in the hunting field—and it is seldom necessary. Of course, a loud voice with lots of carry is required in major circuit bird dog trials where the wide-ranging performer may be quite a long distance from the handler, and it is necessary to bellow to keep contact with the dog. This "hollering business" on the part of professional handlers prompted an amusing observation on the part of an English sportsman attending some of the southern quail trials.

Over in England, all competitors in field trials handle their dogs quietly, sedately. It must be understood that on the other side of the Atlantic, all of the dogs, including pointers and setters, are obliged to stay within a very limited range, and it is a natural corollary that the hunting dogs of Great Britain are under such control that practically all of them can be handled by a motion of the hand. The British gun dogs are more mechanical in their performance than American hunting dogs, but the shooting conditions found in each country may be said to be largely responsible for the differences noted.

In any event, at English field trials there is never a noisy demonstration on the part of the handler, consequently when William Humphrey, noted setter breeder and spaniel authority of Shrewsbury, England, attended the National Championship for pointers and setters at Grand Junction, Tennessee, early in 1926, during the course of a brace when one of the handlers was particularly noisy, he was moved to observe:

"Why does 'e do all that shoutin'? 'E 'ollers when 'e sees 'im and 'e 'ollers when 'e doesn't see 'im! The bloomin' beggar wouldn't get very far in my country with all that 'ollerin', you know."

It must be conceded that sometimes it may be necessary in the case of a wide-ranging field trial setter or pointer to do more or less whistling or shouting, but it is not ordinarily a technique to be recommended.

When we speak of constant shouting and whooping at a dog by a handler, we bring to mind the "driven" dog. This refers particularly to setters and pointers, especially field trial performers that are sometimes described as "made" dogs, meaning that their pace and range are the result of artificial methods and not an exemplification of natural qualifications. In a few words, the breaker by use of voice, whistle, whip, stones, sling shot, or other effective device, gets the dog to remain out at a distance, running hard, but seldom searching for game as he should be doing. He is too intent on keeping a "safe" distance from his handler. Such dogs, incidentally, do not seem to enjoy the "come in" order for fear they may be misinterpreting it. Don't be guilty of driving your dogs out artificially. It makes a bad impression on your shooting friends if they know the difference, and certainly it doesn't deceive any field trial judge who is expert in analyzing class performance and knows when a dog is hunting of its own volition or is constantly being driven away by threatening tactics.

Don't become one of those trainers who constantly admonishes his dog or continually offers encouragement. Some breakers keep it up monotonously with such phrases as "Get away, boy," "Atta boy," "That's the baby," and equally nonsensical terms. Giving too many orders takes the dog's mind off of the real business of hunting. If your dog has natural hunting ability, it can be developed by normal means; on the other hand, if it is necessary to crank him up with a lot of whooping, then something is decidedly wrong with the dog and it would be much better to discard this kind and get one that will go out and do the job naturally.

CHAPTER XII

Introducing the Firearm

Authors of books on the training of hunting dogs are prolix in their warnings. The ambitious amateur who undertakes to train his own shooting dog is cautioned to be careful so that his pupil will not develop certain undesirable habits, the breaker adjured to watch jealously over the reflexes and reactions of the individual dog so that his development will be along right lines. It is not the purpose of this author to lengthen the list of things that must be guarded against, but too much emphasis cannot be placed on the importance of proper introduction of the gun. *Gun-shyness is an acquired trait.* The veteran handler is convinced of this. You may find a few breakers who will claim that fear of the gun is hereditary, but such a premise has been disproved in countless instances. True, the nervous organization of individual dogs may seem to predispose them to gun-shyness, but there is good ground to believe that if the firearm is properly introduced, no hunting dog, even those of otherwise excessive timidity, will develop dread of the gun. This is a pertinent case where doing the thing right in the first place will eliminate a world of difficulty later. It is possible to cure gun-shyness in a sporting dog—just as other cardinal faults with time and intelligent treatment can be overcome—but it is far, far and away much easier to prevent gun-shyness from developing.

Two methods of introducing the firearm are available. Each is predicated on exactly the same principle—having the dog preoccupied with something else so that the report of the gun is merely incidental. One system involves introduction of the gun while the dog is in the field, the other at feeding time. Your aim is to introduce the detonation of a firearm under pleasurable conditions so that the youngster will learn that a gun is not fired for the purpose of scaring him out of a year's growth, and he also perceives that even though bob-white quail, ringneck pheasants, prairie chickens and other game birds may raise a terrible racket when they flush, they do not attack or bite a little doggy.

While the unspoiled pupil, not previously subjected to a scare from shooting or perhaps fireworks noises, is out in the field, dashing here and there, investigating vagrant scents and getting a big kick out of his freedom, carry along a small pistol loaded with blank cartridges which make only a modest report when fired. When the dog suddenly finds game and while he is in the act of chasing, the trainer should let him get some distance away, then snap the pistol. The dog very likely will continue his headlong pursuit without heeding the sound. This is a good token. But in case the dog seems to have been conscious of the noise, if the report causes him to prick his ears, or tuck his tail, or display similar unhappy, fearful emotions, do not by any sign or word take notice of it. To all intents and purposes, the trainer is wholly unconscious of the detonation and if he had been a sufficient distance from the dog and fired when the youngster was busily engaged, at most the puppy will pay slight attention to the noise. After firing, the trainer should immediately pocket the pistol and continue onward as though nothing had happened, regardless of the dog's reaction.

In the event that the detonation makes the dog uneasy, pretend not to notice. In fact, no matter what the dog does, whether he displays timidity, stops hunting, slinks behind you and trails along dejectedly, or whatever might be his tendency, pay not the slightest attention. Under no circumstances try to reassure a dog which shows uneasiness. You may think now that it is simple to act unconcerned, but when actually confronted with the situation it will take firm purpose to keep you from attempting to allay the dog's fears, to pet him and encourage him.

The chances are that if you were a sufficient distance away and the puppy's attention occupied when you shot, your canine pupil will continue whatever he was doing. This is not your cue to hurry things, however; *make haste slowly.* Continue shooting the pistol as opportunity affords, gradually lessening the distance you are from the dog and perhaps using a heavier load as the youngster gains experience. Do not be in a hurry to get to a shotgun and a regulation load. It may seem that the puppy is all set for anything when you are able to discharge the pistol right close to him, but it will still pay to proceed with caution. Many a promising young dog has been ruined by a salvo fired over him by thoughtless shooters.

Accustom the dog to the sight of a gun as well as to the sound of it. Familiarity with the firearm will make him realize that it is nothing to be feared. You will be well recompensed for the care you exercise when you develop in your youngster that love of the gun that characterizes the high-class shooting dog.

When your bird dog puppy has progressed so that he is pointing his game, do not shoot over his first points. Let him become used to the birds. There is a very startling whirr as quail take off and the cackles and alarms of various game birds flushing should become familiar to the dog. Later on, after he has pointed and has become accustomed to the birds being flushed, you can shoot from a distance. When you have become firmly convinced that the dog is not shy of game or afraid of the gun, you can consider killing a bird over his point. It is advisable to have an assistant flush the birds while you stand at a little distance and knock one down so that the dog can readily understand that the shotgun is a necessary adjunct to his work in the field.

Do not hastily fire several shots over the youngster or have several guns blaze away simultaneously; have the dog confirmed in his steadiness and practically imperturbable so far as gun reports are concerned before you consider filling the game bag!

Many noted trainers of hunting dogs, Retrievers and spaniels especially, introduce the gun at feeding time. While the dog is in his kennel yard, preferably at his feed pan, a pistol which makes a low report should be fired from quite some distance away, the person who does the shooting preferably out of sight of the dog. It is desirable if you can observe the dog's reaction without being seen by the dog, but in case you are in the kennel pen, merely go about your business in ordinary fashion, whether or not the dog takes notice of the noise. The procedure is similar to that followed in the field. While the dog is preoccupied with eating, the pistol is fired, the shooter gradually lessening the distance until the dog will not look up from his pan even though the detonation is close by. Use of this method accustoms the dog to the report and is tied in with field shooting as explained previously.

No gun-shyness here! An Irish Setter shows his dependency on the firearms ...

A method advocated by many noted authorities and practiced by successful professional trainers includes having the gun in plain sight at feeding time, permitting the dog to have portions of his meal while interspersing some shooting. Our good friend, Señor J. A. Sanchez Antuñano, who commands the respect and admiration of all lovers of good hunting dogs, in his able and excellent "Practical Education of the Bird Dog," describes the procedure about as follows.

The instructor, carrying a pistol and a packet of food, displays the food to the dog, which has been kept fasting while enclosed in his run. The dog is not allowed to taste the food, but the pan is placed in plain sight, just out of the animal's reach. While the dog strains to reach it, the handler takes a morsel which he gives to him; at the same time the trainer loads the pistol. Moving about twenty yards from the dog, the trainer fires, then immediately goes back to the animal and gives him another bite of food. If the dog shows signs of nervousness, continue firing at the same distance; after a while, go slowly, step by step, toward him, shooting at each point until you are firing near him without any signs of dread on his part. After each report of the gun, give the dog another mouthful of food.

The lesson is repeated the next day, firing and giving the dog mouthfuls of food at short intervals until the dog can tolerate detonations without any signs of uneasiness.

CURE OF GUN-SHYNESS

A gun-shy hunting dog is worthless in the shooting field. The trainer cannot exhibit too great a zeal in endeavoring to avoid gun-shyness in his pupil. If the firearm is properly introduced, there is little danger of this fault developing afterwards. But suppose you are confronted with a gun-shy dog. . . .

Gun-shyness occurs in various degrees and is manifested in many different ways. At the report of a gun, the dog may immediately cease hunting and return to his trainer, getting at heel and following with tail tucked, and he will not—or can he be induced to—resume hunting. This is a more exaggerated form than the dog in that stage which causes him to stop searching at the sound of the gun, trail along at heel for a spell, then his inherent zest for hunting induces him to go out and range once more. The latter case is generally not extremely difficult to overcome. The first type described, however, constitutes more of a problem, though not entirely hopeless. A third type is the dog which at the time the shot is fired, drops his tail and scats for home. The amateur trainer might save himself wear and tear on his patience and perchance ruin of a pleasant disposition if he does not undertake to cure gun-shyness in this third and worst form; it is not impossible, but it is a tedious job even for the specialist.

Gun-shyness, in mild or severe form, can only be overcome by making the dog realize that there is nothing for him to fear in the noise and that actually the shot may contribute to the fun and perhaps procure food. When the dog shows only a slight distaste for the detonation, you can excite his interest by killing a bird for him. While he is off to the side searching, try to flush a bird on your own account and kill it. Hope that the dog sees the "fall," and if he does, you seemingly abandon your sanity. Lay your gun down and run eagerly toward the fallen bird. Try to communicate a share of excitement to the dog. Pick the bird up, toss it in the air, keep playing with it in an effort to awaken the dog's interest. But don't talk to your pupil. Just seem so engrossed in the bird that the dog also naturally wants to take some part in the fun. It may be that the dog will start to hunt thereabouts; if he does not, walk away from this spot and when he has resumed searching elsewhere, swing back to the birds and endeavor to kill a second one. Dash in once more and repeat your previous performance. Upon your talent as an actor, your ability to sway your canine audience will depend your degree of success. In mild cases of gun-shyness, the dog undoubtedly will perk up in interest quite promptly, and from then on, by proceeding with care, you will conquer this ruinous fault.

If you want to tackle difficult cases of gun-shyness—and certainly it is the opinion of this writer that in the case of firearm introduction an ounce of prevention is worth at least several pounds of cure—you have to steel yourself to get results. The most popular method is an adaptation of the "shoot at feeding time" system described as one means of introducing the firearm. That is to say, when your dog approaches his feeding pan, you have someone shoot a light load at a considerable distance; of course, the timorous dog will at once dive back to the innermost recesses of his kennel. The food is promptly removed. The next day at the regular feeding time, the same procedure is followed. If the dog again deserts his feed pen at the detonation and does not soon show signs of returning to it, remove it once more. Driven by hunger, it is very likely that the dog may howl mournfully for his food, but the breaker simply must be hard-hearted. On the third day, pity may well up in your breast for the dog, but under no circumstances may you relent. It is seldom, indeed, that any dog, no matter how severe the case of gun-shyness,

The professional trainer, Dewey English, prepares to shoot over two Pointers

will go very long without food. We have known of some exceptional cases which had to be starved a whole week—and the condition of these dogs rather wrung our heart—but ordinarily this will not be necessary. You will notice that after having no food for a couple of days, while the dog may back into his kennel at the sound of the gun, he will soon poke his head out again and shortly once more approach the feed pan. As he begins to eat, have the gun fired again. Back into the kennel the dog will scoot, but it will not be long until his head reappears and he surveys the situation speculatively. He may be a trifle diffident in his approach to the feed pan this time. but when he has begun to gulp his food once again, have another blank fired. More than likely the retreat this time will be only part way to the kennel, for with hunger gnawing at his vitals and a natural voraciousness militating against fear of the noise, he will stop to look the landscape over, and rather promptly go back to resume feeding. Again the shot; this time, perhaps, the dog only raises his head—and soon he will be so preoccupied with satisfying a ravenous hunger that he will pay no attention to the detonation. You will have accomplished an important stride in the treatment of gunshyness. With the exercise of due care, you will in the course of time entirely overcome the fault.

The J.A.S.A. method advocated in such cases parallels the treatment just described, except that the hungry dog is shown the gun and the pan of food, being permitted to gulp a mouthful. If the sight of the firearm causes the animal to retreat to his kennel, the food is removed. When hunger is sufficiently acute to overcome the dog's fear of the sight of the gun, he is permitted to gulp a mouthful. Then, with the dog tied, the feed pan is placed just out of his reach, the trainer retires about forty or fifty feet, then fires a shot, facing away from the dog. The trainer then goes at once to the dog and gives him a bit of food. Retiring an adequate distance, he fires again, returns and gives the dog additional food. The animal, now ravenous, may want to gulp the entire panful, but each time it is placed just out of his range. Driven by the pangs of hunger, the dog is not likely to exhibit fear of the gun firing. But if after each detonation he seems to be highly nervous and shaking, the trainer should retire a greater distance before shooting. By means of a meager diet to keep the dog's appetite keen, and by assiduous adherence to this procedure, the fault is overcome.

When the dog is taken to the field, a collar and check cord should be attached, the trainer carrying a supply of food, which he has shown to the dog before stuffing it into his jacket. A morsel should be tossed to one side and just as the dog is eating this, the gun fired. If the animal attempts to run off, he will be restrained by the check cord held in your hand or attached to your belt, and other pieces of food should be dropped near the trainer. The dog undoubtedly will shortly come and commence eating these. While he is thus engaged, from a few feet the handler may fire again, meanwhile renewing the food supply, and soon the gun and the detonation are associated in the mind of the dog with a gastronomic reward, and it will be noted that the dog is quick to look about inquiringly at the sound of the gun. Now if you manage to kill a game bird which he had found, you are close to complete success, with only intelligent care and experience needed to complete the cure.

It may be added that certain "cures" take more quickly with individual dogs. The "starvation system" is effective, but has the drawback of keeping the dog from food, perhaps for a period that may seriously affect his physical condition; besides, it is mighty trying on the breaker as well. If you are confronted with a bad case of gun-shyness, study the individual dog and you may be able to devise some system which will prove effective in his case. Some "specialists" have a treadmill in a small room and the dog, reduced to physical exhaustion by his own efforts, finally is persuaded that the gun report is harmless to him.

We recall the instance of the man who took his dog into the woods, then suddenly fired a gun, ran like a madman several yards ahead, stopped to pick something up and then began eating a sandwich which he had surreptitiously taken from his pocket, uttering exclamations of delight and satisfaction. He had come prepared with a concealed lunch and every time he fired the gun, he ran forward, then stopped to eat, endeavoring to convey to the dog that the detonation was responsible for getting the food. While the canine remained coldly aloof from such goings-on at the outset, after a while he began to exhibit some interest, and when he came up quickly to his master after a short sprint, the dog was given a choice bit of food. The very next episode found the dog right at his master's heels—and another morsel rewarded him. It was not long until the idea percolated in the canine cerebellum—*nothing to fear about the gun noise; in fact, it made food available*—and, behold, another case of gun-shyness was practically cured.

Still another classic example of a complete remedy is related of the Chesapeake Bay Dog which, taken out in a boat well to the middle of a large lake, immediately plunged over the side when a gun was fired by his master. The owner pretended no concern. After swimming around for a spell, the Chesapeake returned to the side of the boat in an effort to clamber aboard. He was politely assisted in. A second shot was fired, and the Chessy took to the water once more. The playlet continued along the same lines until the Chesapeake seemed almost exhausted and after his umptieth dive from the boat some alarm was felt lest even so skilled a swimmer might drown. It was a case of sticking to a set formula. The dog eventually concluded that the danger of drowning in his exhausted condition was more to be feared than the report of the gun and so he finally stayed aboard—another victory for persistency!

Ed Farrior, the Alabama professional bird dog handler, who developed and trained such celebrated winners and champions as

Three Chesapeakes and a Flat-Coated Retriever

Doctor Blue Willing, Air Pilot's Sam, Jess Reynolds Diamond, and a host of others, recently related that he had several young dogs develop gun-shyness. They had been farmed out, it seems, and when returned to Farrior he quickly discovered their fear of the firearm. "I started what I called my gun-shy class," explained this noted trainer. "I put the youngsters in crates and carted them along on the dog wagon while we went gunning with old dogs. When one of the seasoned dogs pointed, I had the driver of the wagon get in a position so that the gun-shy pups could see from their crates what was going on. We would flush the birds, kill one or two, and have them retrieved. Without pretending to notice, I observed that after a little bit the youngsters began to take some interest in what was going on and displayed a restlessness to get out of confinement when they saw one of the old dogs on point. I then had leads put on them and let them out of the crates, but kept each a safe distance behind the pointing dog, where the shooting took place. Their interest rapidly increased and they exhibited great eagerness to be in on the fun, and do you know that when we finally let them take part, not one of the youngsters showed the faintest sign of gun-shyness."

Er Shelley had described a somewhat similar procedure in his excellent book, "Twentieth Century Bird Dog Training."

CHAPTER XIII

Early Lessons in the Hunting Field

While the dog is being given his course of instruction in yard training, it is well to grant him frequent romps in the field, where his knowledge of running and ranging may be enlarged. Let the dog have a generally good time; this keeps his spirits up and promotes a keenness for hunting.

There is always much to-do about the best lesson for a puppy and when the breaker should endeavor to exercise control over his pupil in the field. Actually, as has been pointed out earlier in this book, it is desirable to let the youngster get intimately acquainted with a hunting environment. One does not have to go through any elaborate routine with a pedigreed sporting dog—the desirable instincts and character are bred into him, and one with a wealth of natural qualities can make a great trainer out of any one who has sense enough to let the dog's talents and potentialities develop naturally.

As an example of an easy way of starting your prospect, we include here the technique adopted by Clyde Morton of Alberta, Alabama, whose sensational record in top flight competition has stamped him as one of the greatest trainers of class bird dogs in the world, acknowledged to be one of the best in the history of pointer and setter field trials. Interviewing Clyde Morton about his methods, resulted in the following observations by him.

"The first thing I do with a puppy is try to get him to hunt instead of running only. This is done by taking him to the heavy birdy places, such as fencerows, plum thickets, pea patches, etc. If he begins to show that he wants to reach out, then I start giving him the whistle signals. When he starts back to me, I always face him, using a sharp blow on the whistle, and keep it up until I get him turned away again. I believe this is where lots of pups start going wrong. I have seen puppies turn to go home or to the wagon, others come to the horse and go all the way around him, then out again.

Photo by W. Eugene Smith
Taken to the hunting field in the dog wagon, this Pointer is eager to get going as he is unloaded by the trainer's helper

I have stopped plenty of them from these things by facing them no matter what direction they came in from, using the whistle until they turned away again. If they start back, I repeat the performance until the pup will turn as soon as he hears the sharp blow. I will admit that there are a few pups which never get this into their heads.

"In turning a pup to the whistle, I use a longer blow and generally two. If a pup hears the first and stops to locate the sound, he will catch the second signal. If he is in sight, you can give him the turning blast and most of the time he will go on.

"I have never used a whistle in yard-breaking my dogs. I think a field trial dog should be taught as few signals as possible. This helps to keep other handlers who might keep up a continual whistling and yelling from confusing your dogs.

"I have seen handlers catch a dog in the collar, give him a cut across the back with the whip and at the same time give a sharp blow on the whistle. This procedure produces what I call a whip-runner or whistle-runner, and a dog will exhibit it every time his handler shows up. I never use a whip except for punishment and when this is necessary I never let the dog go until I have made friends with it.

"When starting a pup, I never shoot over his first points. I let him get used to the birds first, then I shoot from my horse when the dog is nearby so that he can see there is no harm in the gun. After this has been done a few times and I am sure he is not afraid of the birds or of the gun, I let my helper flush the birds and I stand at a distance and shoot at the same time the birds are flushed, killing a bird and making the helper hold the pup steady with a check cord. When this has been done a few times, I will walk in, flush the birds, wait until they are almost out of sight, then fire the gun, making him stand all of this time. I have always found it best never to let the youngster break shot, even at the beginning of his training, excepting the puppy which is inclined to be timid. Some trainers claim a dog is born gun-shy. I have not found this to be true, and can count all the gun-shy pups I've had on one hand."

There is nothing that need be added to Clyde Morton's observations. The success he has attained bespeaks his individual skill as well as the effectiveness of his system. It should be said that the Alabama professional stresses the fact that dogs must be trained as individuals. "You have to know the dog, become familiar with his temperament and character, get to know what he can do and what you can do with him, and only the trainer who is able to devise some scheme for getting the idea across to his dog when confronted by a special problem is going to develop consistently real high-class performers. You must always be alert in the hunting field and adapt your methods to the disposition, character, and courage of the dog, any peculiarities he may have, and it is always of utmost importance to retain the dog's complete confidence in you."

It does seem worthwhile to supplement Clyde Morton's remarks

Photo by W. Eugene Smith
A young Pointer is cut loose on the Canadian prairies

by saying that his practice of never letting the youngster break shot is not adhered to by all the leading professional bird dog handlers. Jake Bishop of Union Springs, Alabama, a grand veteran and one of the ranking trainers over a long period of years, who has always been noted for the beautiful manner in which he polishes his dogs on game, believes that by permitting the dogs to break shot occasionally, it keeps them keener, inclined to display greater fervency on point, and because he finds it an easy matter to keep them steady when he so wills, he sometimes encourages a dog to break shot in order to maintain the dog's zest at high pitch.

"I find that it does some dogs a lot of good to let them break shot occasionally," Jake Bishop has told us, "and even with some of the old dogs, it keeps them more fiery in their pointing attitudes. Of course, in workouts just prior to any field trial competition, we have the dog steady as a rock on his game; the main thing is to get the idea across to the dog that it can be lots of fun and you let him enjoy it to the utmost, and that there are other occasions that are serious business and he is expected to exhibit his best manners. You can draw a parallel with people. Most of us do not always want to have to display 'drawing room' etiquette when we would be more comfortable in our shirt-sleeves if the situation permitted."

For the sake of the record, it is put down here that the vast majority of professional trainers, and practically all authors of books on the training of hunting dogs, strongly advise that once the dog has established a point, the handler should, if it is at all possible, prevent the dog from chasing. Jake Bishop's technique has proved very successful in his experience and the reader can approach this phase of dog training with confidence if the dog is given individual consideration according to its own temperament.

While the foregoing applies particularly to the pointing breeds, and especially to the development of field trial dogs, much of what was said is equally applicable to spaniels and Retrievers. Take them out, let their natural instincts ripen, do not rush their education in the refinements of training, and watch for the exact moment when you can begin to control their activities in the hunting field. The greater the dog's keenness for searching out game, the more valuable he will prove and the more readily will he assimilate the various lessons you will give him.

CHAPTER XIV

Lessons in Retrieving

In the case of the pointing breeds, it is not recommended that you hasten this part of your prospect's education. While retrieving may be taught by the force method any time after the youngster is ten months of age, in the case of setters and pointers it is preferred to have them benefit by a season in the hunting field before schooling them in the art of retrieving. This does not apply to the same extent to the spaniels and of course not at all to the recognized Retriever breeds, where contrary to the opinions of many, we believe it an entirely natural rather than artificial quality; at least, the Retrievers seem to do it properly almost instinctively. If it is not instinct with them, certainly it may be termed predisposition.

For the lessons in retrieving, you can select any season of the year you may wish. We have always taken the view that the warm weather provides a welcome interlude for the bird hunter to yard train his puppy and teach his dog to fetch. During the Summer, opportunity to work dogs afield is not practical. Vegetation is green, high and rank; the shooting season is closed; conditions generally are unfavorable. But the time need not be lost. It may be used to advantage for obedience training of sporting dogs. An owner may profitably spend the months of warm weather preparing for the coming of the Fall and glorious days afield in quest of wary, elusive game birds. It is, we repeat, a chance to yard-break his dog and give elementary lessons in force retrieving. Many dogs learn to retrieve in a spirit of play, but authorities generally agree that the force-taught retriever is most reliable.

It is a natural reaction for a hunting dog, any breed in fact, to find enjoyment in the pursuit of any object which moves along the

112

ground. Watch the glee of a puppy as he chases a ball! This tendency may be used to advantage if the "play method" is used for teaching the dog to retrieve. Some excellent performers result from inducing the dog to fetch merely as a diversion, without use of any force whatsoever. But in the event that a dog which retrieves "for the fun of it," decides in the field that he does not want to fetch a dead or crippled bird, the shooter is at a loss for means of accomplishing this purpose. However, if the dog has been put through a course of force retrieving, his obedience under any and all circumstances may be gained.

It should be reiterated that in the case of recognized Retrievers and of spaniels, too, retrieving propensities are more highly developed than in other breeds, hence some of the steps outlined in this chapter need not be resorted to in the instance of Labrador Retrievers, Chesapeake Bay Dogs, etc.

It is a long time since retrieving was a requisite quality of the successful performer in pointer and setter trials. Years ago, it was the plaintive wail of handlers that if required to break their dogs to retrieve, they would risk taking much of the spirit and dash out of them, that it would detract from the qualities defined as *class* and perhaps retard their development as outstandingly bold-going field trial performers. At all events, so far as pointer and setter trials go, retrieving has been consigned to the discard, but the gunner will find this a most important accomplishment in his shooting dog. Besides, conservation authorities have been stressing the value of a good retriever. Not a few dead and many crippled upland game birds, wild-fowl or even other game are lost because of lack of the services of a good retrieving dog. To the conscientious sportsman, it is most annoying to lose a crippled bird, and our wild-life resources would be greatly conserved if all shooters were accompanied by crack retrievers.

Teaching a dog to fetch requires a thorough understanding of the art on the part of the educator to prevent restriction of the dog's natural qualities. While spaniels and the regular Retrievers have an instinctive flair for it, there is no gainsaying that setters and pointers can become very accomplished in the art, as do the balance of the pointing breeds.

Retrieving is a necessary part of the training of a shooting dog, especially where the owner keeps only one dog to gun over. If, as some sportsfolk practice in the South, a kennel harbors a variety of sporting breeds so that the laird of the manor can take pointers and setters to find and stand the game, plus spaniels or Retrievers at heel to recover the birds which are dropped, one need not worry about teaching the pointing dogs to seek dead and retrieve, but few are situated so happily.

There have been different systems of force retrieving in vogue in days gone by and we do not doubt that nearly all of them are still being used with great effectiveness. Any person with a reasonable amount of patience and firmness, who has had some experience in handling dogs, can break a dog to retrieve. But unless the instructor is resolved to carry through the entire course of force retrieving, he should not attempt any part of it. Each of the progressive steps is essential and must be followed in the proper order. The length of time that may be required to teach different dogs to retrieve will vary considerably. Some canines will absorb the lessons in a very short time, others acquire skill very slowly. But no matter how timid or headstrong a dog may be, sooner or later he will submit if the instructor employs an effective system.

The J.A.S.A. Force Collar is recommended. Care must be exercised in its use. Because pain is inflicted to coerce the dog, the trainer must be sufficiently expert in the use of the collar so that as soon as the dog obeys (does what is required of him), the pressure ceases immediately. Many a dog may be cowed by use of the force collar in the hands of a novice or thoughtless breaker, but if intelligently and skillfully used, it is a training aid of immeasurable value.

While we have recommended the J.A.S.A. collar, it should be explained that you may take your choice of various means (all based on inflicting pain) to make the dog open his mouth, and certain dogs seem to respond to one way better than to others. For example, use of the force collar; pressing the dog's lips against his fangs; pinching his ear, or applying pressure to one of the dog's paws. Choose any of them or a combination, a few breakers resorting to the collar and ear pinching in the case of obstinate dogs.

A great many professional trainers still adhere to the old Dave Sanborn system, which calls for the breaker to hold the article in one hand, taking one of the dog's forepaws in the other, apply pressure to the paw until the dog opens his jaws, then quickly slip

Photo by W. Eugene Smith
One method of forcing dog to open jaws to receive game

the object into the dog's mouth and place the left hand under his chin. Punishment must cease just as soon as the dog complies.

If you prefer to press the animal's lips against his fangs, hold the retrieving object, which is usually a corncob, in your right hand in front of the dog's mouth. With your left hand, take hold of the dog's head just under the eyes, across the bridge, then press the upper lips between the dog's teeth. This will force the dog to open his jaws.

If you pinch the ear—*do not pull it*—merely place your thumb on the inside and press against the forefinger on the other side.

If use is made of the J.A.S.A. collar, place it on the dog so that the buckle is under the throat, the dog is sitting in front of you. Take hold of the collar near the buckle with your right hand, keep the object in front and over his mouth. Order "Fetch," and at the same time pull his collar up toward the object. When the dog opens

Holding the object for dog to take

his mouth, immediately release the pressure as you slip the article between his teeth.

Lessons in retrieving should be short. A few minutes will suffice ordinarily for mastery of a step, but under no circumstances should the training be prolonged beyond a quarter hour, though the sessions may be frequent.

The initial lesson, of course, is to teach the dog to open his mouth so you can put an object in; next, to prevail on him to hold the object after it has been placed in his mouth and to carry the same; third, to take it from your hand; fourth, to pick it up from the ground; fifth, to go a distance and get it; sixth, to retrieve it to your hand. Each of these acts are steps in educating a dog to retrieve and each must be forced separately in sequence. You might throw down an object and pull a dog's head brutally trying to make him pick it up, but you can quite humanely place an object in his mouth and compel him to hold it by the method suggested. When you check him, he soon learns to open his mouth at command, and by repetition of each step as the dog progresses, he is brought to real proficiency.

When the dog has retrieved, he should come directly in front of you and sit up on his haunches, holding the cob in his mouth until you take it from him. He has been taught to sit in the course of yard breaking and in the lesson, "Coming When Called," it was explained how, if the pupil was inclined to stop several feet in front of you, you could induce him to advance rapidly and close up.

Placing object in dog's mouth

You can get your dog to assume a sitting position directly in front and near at hand by feeding him choice morsels; occasionally step back a few feet to make it necessary for him to follow you. A few sessions and the canine pupil will understand his obligation to approach you closely.

Select your "schoolroom" or place of instruction carefully, with an eye and ear to the absence of any distractions. You may decide on a small, quiet room barren of furnishings or a secluded yard where interruptions will not occur. Since the dog has already been made familiar with the force collar and has learned its persuasive power, put it on and make him sit up in front of you, then follow quickly when you step back a few feet. If he does not start promptly with you, check him lightly. He will soon pay strict attention. Then walk away several paces, turn and call him to you, and while he sits up directly in front, place the article in his mouth. The object, by the way, should be something lightweight, about eight inches long and two inches in diameter. Select an article that seems to interest the dog. Suitable suggestions include a good-sized corncob stripped of its kernels; a portion of a broom-stick handle, covered with cloth; a bit of rubber hose; or similar object that can be readily thrust into the dog's mouth and one which he can hold properly.   Later a heavier object may be substituted.

With the dog sitting in proper position, you check him to open his mouth, slip the article between his teeth and place your left hand under his lower jaw. Simultaneous with the application of the

Trainer has had dog hold object while he walked a distance ahead

force, you command "Fetch," and release the pressure instantly when the dog parts his jaws and you press the article between his teeth. You can count on the dog promptly endeavoring to get rid of the object. Do not force the issue at the outset. Patience is called for—and repetition! But by having hold of one end, you can keep the article in the dog's mouth. If he succeeds in dropping it, merely replace the article and repeat until the dog seems to realize what is expected of him. Then, if he drops it after you have put it in his mouth, check him for it, replace it, and check him each time he drops it. This checking should be done while the dog is in the act of ejecting the article. Endeavor to anticipate him so that there is unmistakable association of ideas, the dog understanding that the command, "Fetch," and the order, "Hold," when obeyed, eliminate the force. It is even likely that before the first short lesson is at an end, the dog will readily reach out to take the article when it is shown to him.

About five or six minutes is time enough for this lesson and remember that no session should be prolonged unduly, and that each should have an enjoyable diversion afterwards. You want to keep the dog cheerful, his interest keen, and disposed to take a real part in what is being done.

The next time you put the collar on, have the dog hold the article,

Setter is encouraged to deliver article

then lead him about with it in his mouth. While he was doing splendidly when sitting or standing with it in his mouth, just as soon as you require him to carry it, he will surely drop it once he is in motion. This is not stubbornness, but just a lack of co-ordination. Follow the procedure outlined in connection with the first step. Replace the article patiently until he understands what is wanted, then check him each time he drops it; be firm but not severe. Soon you will have him following you rather proudly with the article in his mouth. Most dogs are quick to absorb this lesson and seem to get a great deal of satisfaction from it. In fact, when you seek to take the article from the pupil's mouth after he has been carrying it, he will be loath to let go of it, evidence that you have made some impression on him. Just voice the command, "Let go," holding your hand under the dog's mouth. Remove it carefully by opening his mouth gently and taking the article from him. It is preferable that he hold it steadily until you are ready to receive it rather than exhibit a tendency to drop it quickly.

When you have the dog holding the article and carrying it well without any inclination to drop it, you are ready for the third step. Endeavor to get the dog to take the article from your hand. He may have showed signs of doing this in the first lesson and little difficulty should be encountered. Hold the article close in front of

A heavier article is substituted

his mouth, order "Go fetch," and check him slightly; assist him in every way possible to take the article from your hand. If he merely stretches his neck and opens his mouth, but does not grasp the article, put it into his mouth and gradually encourage him to do the whole job of his own volition. When you succeed in getting him so that he will snatch it from your hand, allow him to hold it and follow you about with it in his mouth, and praise him. Have him sit in the proper position before voicing the order, "Let go," and stroke him gently when you take the object from him. You gradually increase the distance the dog will take the article from your hand, and when he will promptly attempt to take it at a distance of three feet, move it away still farther as he endeavors to get it, this in order to induce the dog to keep his eye on the article and follow it. Actually, the dog will be directed by your hand, and you can now proceed to hold the article at different levels. This should be done by easy stages, a little above the level of the dog's head, then a bit lower, and slightly to the sides. If he refuses to take it from a certain place, go back to the previous position and drill the dog until he becomes accustomed to taking it from wherever it is held.

The fourth step is one that may require sublime patience and the trainer should not endeavor to hurry through this. It may be well, also, to substitute for the article being used—corncob, portion of

Dog approaches carrying the heavy article

broom-stick handle, leather glove, length of rubber hose—the saw-buck, previously described under "Implements of Training." While some breakers continue to use a corncob for this lesson, substitution of the sawbuck will facilitate the dog's picking up of the article from the ground and also teach him to grasp objects in the center and not at the ends. Clean, quick pick-ups come with practice. Incidentally, after the first few steps have been mastered by the dog, the trainer may prefer to change to different contrivances so that the dog will not become obsessed with the idea that he is in duty bound to confine his act to the single type of object. If the dog refuses the substitute, merely go through the succession of steps until he arrives at the proper stage of his advancement.

Have him take the sawbuck from directly in front of his nose, then gradually lower it until you place it on the ground. If at any time you get it so low that he does not condescend to take it, revert to the previous position and descend by easy levels. When you finally place it on the ground, keep your hand alongside it, because if you take your hand away, his eye may follow your hand and be misguided by it. If the dog happens to be awkward in his initial attempts to pick up the sawbuck, which is unlikely if he has been well drilled in previous steps, render such assistance as you deem necessary. When the dog reaches the stage where he will perform the chore graciously, gradually draw away your hand, a little farther each time, until the pupil picks up the article without paying any attention to the position of your hand.   It is important that each lesson be learned thoroughly before going on to the next.

The fifth step is a logical sequel to the previous lesson. Hold the article out in front of the dog to take; if he does not grab it, check him. As soon as he is conforming promptly, drop the sawbuck on the ground close in front of the dog and entice him to pick it up. When he does, take it from him, then as he follows you to get it again, let it drop on the ground in front of him, suiting the distance to the particular case. The dog may readily go six feet more or less and do his part nicely, or again he may try to pick it up hurriedly, miss it and become disinterested. Do not be overly critical so long as the dog makes a proper effort. Walk with him, repeat the order, "Go fetch," and, if essential to his success, assist him a little, but do not overdo the assistance part. It may be necessary in the early instruction of this lesson to accompany the dog to the object several times before ordering him to go alone. Don't stop accompanying him abruptly. Toss the sawbuck here and there, start toward it with the dog each time as if you were going along then stop. You now reach the sixth step, wherein the check cord may prove of great assistance. Have him return with the article, sit up and hold it. If he is disposed to drop it before you give the order, "Let go," force him to hold it steadily until you voice the command. Be firm in this portion of the instruction. You want the dog to be a classy retriever and to do his job in polished style, so be sure that he approaches closely, sits alertly, holds the article without fidgeting and releases it promptly at the spoken order and the sign with your hand, which will consist of placing your hand beneath the dog's mouth. In the event the dog is reluctant to release the article, there are different ways of forcing him to open his mouth, but we suggest that of stepping on one of his forepaws. He will be in sitting position and you can easily apply pressure on a paw with your foot.

These steps are also preliminary to teaching the dog to mark. By having his gaze follow the object as you toss it out, his eye is sharpened, his judgment of distance, even though these tosses are short, may be noted, albeit you will give additional schooling in "marking" under conditions better suited to the purpose, as explained in the succeeding chapter.

CHAPTER XV

Retrieving of Game

When the dog is fully versed in the steps outlined in the preceding chapter, you are ready to adapt what he has learned about the art of retrieving to practical value in the hunting field, on the marsh, or from the blind. The system employed in force retrieving should always consist of methods designed to keep the dog keen. You do not want a timid or cowed dog; you want one that will be a stylist at his work, alert, happy, merry, bringing the game to you on the run, proud of his accomplishment. For this reason, his introduction to the actual retrieving of game should be in a manner calculated to instill a zest in the dog for the sport.

The transition from retrieving such articles as a section of broomstick handle or sawbuck to upland game birds, wild-fowl, and rabbits will be made without confusion. A dead pigeon will also be substituted for articles previously utilized, and you should in fact use upland game birds or ducks so that the dog will have learned to perform in gratifying style when he is actually retrieving for the gun. The experienced trainer introduces sundry devices to be retrieved in the course of the lessons explained previously and comes to the hunting field all prepared for the dog to do his preview stuff with, say, a dead pigeon. When a tame pigeon is sacrificed, it is recommended that you kill it in such a way that no blood flows. If dispatched otherwise, be sure the bird is not mutilated and that all traces of gore are removed from the feathers. The pigeon corpse should be stiff and cold before you commence to use it. It is important that your dog does not become "feather shy." Handlers of Retrievers especially will tell you that many a green dog doesn't fancy having his mouth full of feathers. The smart thing to do when introducing the pigeon to be retrieved is rehearse the various steps, at which time you take notice if the dog has a "tender mouth."

It is imperative that game be delivered tenderly to your hand by the dog, otherwise he cannot be classified as a good retriever. By adroit use of the check cord you can prevent the dog from mauling the bird after he picks it up, but hard mouth demands special treat-

A pair of Pointers retrieve a "double" scored by their proud owner

ment. Should the dog be inclined to bite too roughly, a majority of authorities recommend that a few stiff wires be passed through the bird's body, with the tips sticking out, so that when the dog presses too tightly on the bird, the protruding ends will prompt him to drop it quickly. Though the pupil may be reluctant, he must be forced to take the wired bird and be compelled to carry it until he does the job properly.

Martin J. Hogan, noted trainer of Barrington, Illinois, an expert in the development of non-slip Retrievers, does not resort to the use of wired birds, or eggs with nails protruding, or dummy hares with punishing wire ends. He merely uses a cold, taped pigeon, placing this in the dog's mouth, having the dog take it with the trainer's fingers underneath the bird. Any pressure by the dog results in a sharp rap under his mouth with the trainer's free hand. This method is sufficient in ordinary cases to assure tender handling of the bird by the dog. In case the dog proves of confirmed hard mouth, Mr. Hogan does not attempt to overcome it, but simply abandons training that particular dog. Experience teaches that this is viewing the situation in the proper light, and a similar attitude toward bad gun-

Fox Photos

Cocker Spaniel retrieving rabbit

shy cases, etc., is recommended. It would be better for all concerned to forego any training effort rather than attempt to overcome serious faults. Get good prospects with desirable natural qualities and educate them with a minimum of strife rather than struggle to eradicate major faults. This is not to say that shortcomings and "vices" cannot be corrected, and the prospect made a useful performer, but the amount of effort required to accomplish this does not justify the end!

To return to the original theme of this chapter. First of all in taking the dog to the hunting field for application of the lessons in force retrieving, the pupil should be drilled in "marking." In a sense, marking, like nose, is a natural quality, but with intelligent practice a dog's inherent gift will be enhanced. Marking by a dog consists of his observing the "fall" of game and, when given the order, going quickly to the fall and locating the game readily. Take your canine pupil to an open field where the ground is level and there is no cover to obscure the article to be retrieved. To begin with, have a likely object with sufficient weight to enable you, when wanted, to hurl it some distance away, as far as forty yards. You may think you have to possess an arm like a major league baseball player, but it is difficult to give a Retriever practical experience except in this artificial way.

In the case of a dog of the pointing breeds, he will be standing at your side, whereas if you are educating a spaniel or a non-slip Retriever, the dog will be sitting alertly. Show the object to the dog, then throw it high in the air and some distance away, so that the pupil may see its flight and mark its fall. The dog should be steady, awaiting the order to "Go fetch." The dog will keep his eyes riveted on the location of the object; do not detain him more than momentarily at the outset, and at the order he should go straight to the article at a fast clip, pick it up quickly and return at a snappy pace to the trainer. The conventional spaniel must sit up in front of the instructor and deliver the object to hand. It is optional with a person whether or not his pointing dog sits before delivery or if he will accept it from the dog standing. Many teach their setters and pointers to rear up alongside a horse and release the bird to the master seated in the saddle.

The preliminary work in marking should be done without the dog resorting in the slightest to use of his nose. He should be qualified to mark the fall accurately, the article remaining in sight on the ground, and the dog should go directly to the spot. Note well the dog's judgment of distance, whether he hesitates short of the object or if he overruns it; do not throw it so far at the outset as to cause the dog to hesitate to retrieve the object promptly.

After the dog retrieves an object thrown straight away, start tossing to the right and to the left, hurl it high in the air and then toss it out like a clothes-line, accustoming the dog to watch the flight at any and all levels. When the dog will mark accurately and go quickly in a straight line to the spot—anywhere within gun range—you are ready for the next step. This consists principally of a change of venue—from the flat, open field, where the object remained in plain sight, to terrain not so favorable for marking purposes. There are two objectives: (a) the dog must learn from experience to co-ordinate his movements under more difficult ground conditions; (b) he must come to understand that not only is he called upon to mark as closely as possible the exact spot where the fall occurred, but that he is obliged to go there swiftly and seek in a brisk albeit quiet manner, using his nose to advantage as he quarters thoroughly the immediate area.

The trainer will, consequently, toss the object on the edge of

A Pointer retrieves dead quail

cover, then throw it farther in so that it will not be in sight. He will encourage in the dog reliance on his nose after he has reached the spot he marked with his eyes! Make this work as simple as possible at the start, gradually requiring more of the pupil and it will not be long until the dog should be able to mark accurately, find quickly and retrieve promptly.

A chunk of liver, fried very hard in butter or lard, may be introduced in these lessons. Let the dog smell it, tantalize him slightly, then throw it and let him seek. This will assist in getting him to search enthusiastically. Don't walk up and show him where it is;

if he fails to find it, you go and pick it up, then repeat the per formance. Incidentally, this tossing of the liver chunk teaches the dog certain signals; viz., that a motion of the arm to the right means there is something good to be found in that direction and he can get it by using his nose; likewise to the left and forward.

The next step will test the capacity of your pupil for advancement. You may feint with the object in one direction, then toss it in an other, and finally you will conceal it in a spot unobserved by the

Photo by W. Eugene Smith
Labrador Retriever makes a prompt return with duck

dog. Now the order will be, "Dead; fetch." Your purpose is twofold: (1) to have your dog accept directions from your motions with an arm when he has not actually marked the fall, and (2) to accustom your dog to search with his nose for dead or crippled game. The practical sportsman realizes that for real success as a retriever, the pointing dog must adopt a different technique than that he uses in hunting for live game, when he should seek body scent, carrying his head high. Whereas, when locating killed or wounded game, best results are achieved by a careful, methodical search, head low and nose close to the ground to catch the scent. The piece of liver can be useful to intensify the dog's diligence, and later you can place a piece on a bush or a low limb of a tree, and encourage the dog to find it so that he may learn that occasionally a dead bird may be found in an unusual place. Use the command, "Dead, fetch," then add "Up," with an inflection of the voice and a hand gesture that will indicate to the dog what is desired of him.

In the case of pointing dogs, care must be taken not to let the dog get in the habit of searching with his nose close to the ground else he may adopt this objectionable form when searching for live game, thus becoming a potterer or grass prowler. It is up to the trainer

Photo by W. Eugene Smith
Labrador Retriever delivers game to hand

to arrange his guidance so that such a contingency does not arise.

Some owners of setters and pointers may prefer not to teach their dogs the art of retrieving, and a few believe it is satisfactory to have the dog locate and point dead game. This can be easily taught, for if the trainer has the dog obedient to the command of "Whoa," he will encounter no difficulty.

Much of what has been written here has no direct application to the recognized Retriever breeds, for their education involves simply taking advantage of natural qualities and tendencies. The education of the Retriever in his particular sphere of action may begin at six or eight weeks and little force is needed. The Retrievers and spaniels will take more readily to the water than the pointing dogs, but the latter can be aquatically trained by tossing choice tidbits out in shallow water where the bottom slopes away gradually to greater depth, like an indoor swimming pool. With a stingy diet as a hunger spur, plus a run which will make the dog hot, he can be induced to go into the water quickly, both because of its appeal as a place of comforting relief and for the pieces of thrown food that float on the surface. The distance these morsels are thrown may be lengthened until the dog is swimming in deep water to get them. Subsequently,

Photo by W. Eugene Smith
Labrador Retriever sits docilely holding pheasant

the dog is taught to retrieve from water, a simple procedure if the pupil has been thoroughly grounded in his retrieving lessons on land.

Spaniels and Retrievers can be schooled in retrieving live game, using a hobbled duck or pigeon for the purpose. A wing clipped duck may also be thrown into a pond and the dog sent after it until the duck is exhausted and the dog succeeds in grasping it. Retrievers should be encouraged to respond to signals from their handlers, take directions readily, and in the training lessons the breaker must be sure that when the dog works properly, the object is retrieved.

Photo by W. Eugene Smith

Working with a Labrador Retriever, a fair Diana has the trainer anxious as she accepts the bird

Never send a dog any place where game has not fallen or been placed; when a Retriever obeys signals and makes a gallant try, he should not be imposed on with a fool's errand.

Although these various steps are outlined at considerable length, the experienced trainer can accomplish his ends without going through quite so monotonous a routine. He has become versed in "short cuts," but the author has purposely avoided dwelling on any of these, because the long way is more likely to be the best way for the amateur. We are reminded of the story of the head gardener on one of the vast estates in England. He had written a book about gardening, one that described fully the ways and means and methods of certain operations. One day a feminine visitor to the gardens watched this man with interest while he had a corps of assistants do certain work. Suddenly the lady said, "You don't do those things exactly as you outline in your book!" "No, madam," replied the gardener, "with all the work to be done, I simply haven't the time. If I did it according to the book, I'd need twice as many men."

The moral is that experience teaches short cuts. That is the way with professional dog trainers. They have a large number of dogs to educate and have found that by study of the individual dog and recognition of his natural qualities, elementary steps may be safely eliminated. As one gains experience in the development and training of hunting dogs, it will be found that a dog's natural inclinations may be taken full advantage of to abridge many of the methods suggested in this book. But do not try to gain skill of this kind too quickly. It is far more difficult to get rid of an error in judgment than to acquire a correct idea in the first instance. There is no royal road to learning; be content to pick up much important information in the slow but sure empirical way.

CHAPTER XVI

Quartering—Hunting to the Gun

Has your hunting dog been given frequent excursions in the field
without any attempt at control? Have you permitted him to become
familiar with hunting environment, allowed him to run independently and search energetically, to flush and pursue sundry small
songsters as well as any upland game birds he may have encountered
in his helter-skelter scampering? After his zest for hunting had become keen and there was evidence of embryonic bird sense—notice
how a puppy expects to find game in situations similar to that in
which he first disturbed birds—did you start him in the yard breaking routine, meanwhile continuing his daily romps in the field where
the bird dog prospect was given full freedom?

Now the obedience lessons which constitute the yard breaking
curriculum have been mastered; perhaps you have also given your
dog complete instruction in the various steps of force retrieving. In
the case of setters and pointers, the retrieving education may be
delayed until after a full season afield, but this is optional with the
trainer. At any rate, you have reached the point in the development
of the dog where you are considering application of the obedience
training to the canine pupil's work in the field. There should be a
review of preceding lessons and you will supplement voice commands with hand and whistle signals.

You have been given some instruction in how to make the dog
"whistle conscious." A single, sharp blast is to signify the same as
the spoken command, "Whoa." It is simple to teach this stop signal.
Place a lead on the dog, walk with him, then give the single toot
and instantly force the dog to halt. If he attempts to move, whistle
and bring him up short. Do this as you stroll around the kennel
yard or other suitable enclosure and the dog will soon comprehend.

134

Freudy Photo

Harry D. Kirkover with a group of his excellent English Setters and Pointers

You can arrange whistle signals to suit yourself. Many trainers use two toots to turn the dog, blowing two sharp notes, one to attract the dog's attention, the second for him to proceed in the particular direction; some use a long blast to get the dog's attention and two toots for "hie on" or "go out." In field trials, handlers use three blasts on the whistle as a signal to scouting assistants that the dog is back on the course or in hand. Rather shrill continuous whistling is used by a few handlers as a sort of "contact" signal, to have the dog look

A brace of bird dogs, Pointer and Setter, get away with a great burst of speed

them up. Jack Harper, developer and handler of the sensational pointer dog, The Texas Ranger, winner of ten championship titles perfected the response of his dog to such trilling notes. Prolonged whistle blowing is also used as the "Come in" signal.

The first phase of field hunting under control will be preliminary education in ground work, educating the dog in the mechanics of quartering or systematic ranging. Specifically, "quartering" may be defined as ranging pendulum fashion in front of the hunter, searching the cover a reasonable distance on both sides and ahead. It is a mechanical process in its strictest sense and while it is imperative that spaniels range methodically, as well as any non-slip Retrievers which are taught to hunt in spaniel fashion, the pointing dogs are allowed more latitude and expected to exhibit "bird sense" in the manner in which they negotiate a field. Not that the spaniels have their "game sense" curbed, but their sphere of activity is limited to gun range. "Bird sense" in pointing dogs implies searching the likely places on the course intelligently without necessarily covering the territory in quartering style.

In the case of all hunting breeds, ranging comes quite naturally and the dogs fall into particular categories—from bold, fast, strong, independent, keen searching, wide-ranging field trial prospects to slow, phlegmatic plug shooting dogs. You had better discard the latter and put your effort in on the ambitious hunter of courage and character.

Teaching a setter or pointer to quarter properly is quite a chore, whereas education of the spaniel in this respect is more readily accomplished. This is because the spaniel is required to stay within shotgun range, his casts not exceeding forty yards, and a lengthy window sash cord can be attached to the collar of the dog to convey to him quickly the idea of quartering. The *modus operandi* is quite simple.

The spaniel puppy is permitted to go out and hunt. More likely than not, he will swing from side to side quite satisfactorily while the handler holds the end of the cord. If the puppy objects to the cord being held, simply let him drag it. In the event he does not want to hunt with a long cord—say thirty or forty feet—attached to his collar, replace this with a shorter one, then gradually increase its length until the dog is dragging as much line as you consider adequate.

As the dog quests off to the right, just when he reaches the distance you have predetermined, check him with the cord and simultaneously sound a distinctive note on your whistle. If the spaniel is trailing the check cord, merely step on it for the desired effect. As the puppy's attention is attracted, immediately start to walk in the opposite direction, at the same time giving a signal by motioning with your arm for the puppy to cross to the left hand side. If the youngster appears confused at first, do not be dismayed. This is a normal reaction. After repetition, the dog will come to understand that the whistle and the simultaneous check signify a turn or change of direction, and when his response is satisfactory you can quit the cord.

Permitted to hunt minus the cord, the puppy, conscious of the absence of this restraining influence, may hesitate when you blow on the whistle, then decide not to obey. This is the moment for the breaker to act. Do not call the dog to you and punish him. Let it be re-emphasized that under no circumstances should a dog be called in and then punished. Go quietly, get the dog and bring him back forcibly to the exact place he was when you blew the whistle. Require him to stay put. Blow the whistle several times and with each note remind the dog with a light tap. Then resume hunting. If the dog does not give proper response to the whistle next time, you can be more emphatic in reminding him that this is serious business. But continual practice is necessary to achieve best results. Do not try to hasten the dog's education in this respect for there is a probability that crowding him will tend to discourage his enthusiastic searching.

In coaching the dog to quarter, do not permit him to cross behind you and be careful to note that turns are made in an outward direction. If the dog turns back toward the handler with an inside loop, he is covering some ground already gone over, hence the trainer should be alert to see that the idea of the forward turn becomes second nature with the dog. The outward turn with the pointing breeds may require careful and at times long-drawn-out instruction, but, just as in the case of quartering, with the spaniel means are at hand to more readily make the dog comprehend what is desired. In case the dog is turning with an inside loop, it may indicate that the handler is lagging, not proceeding on the course fast enough, and by quickening the pace the canine pupil will invariably begin to make the turns correctly.

Once the dog is turning properly and promptly to the whistle, you can direct him to the promising places. If you possess good "game sense" yourself, you can quickly assist your scholar to acquire useful knowledge. While it is true that "game sense" in many dogs is a natural quality that is enriched by experience, nevertheless a trainer who is a shrewd judge of likely game cover can aid the dog's development of this important quality.

A word of caution, however. Do not cultivate a mechanical response in your dog that will make of him a mere automaton. Do not have him continually looking for directions. He is naturally fitted to find the game, and exercise of his own initiative will prove

A Pointer and an English Setter race away in search of bob-white quail

more fruitful than making the dog look constantly to his handler for instructions. We have mentioned before that if the dog does this, his mind is not on what is of principal importance—finding game.

Before we leave special consideration of the spaniel, it might be well to say a few words about handling on running game, either birds or rabbits. When the spaniel's stub tail speeds up, the emotions he expresses indicate that he is on the line of game, or has body scent located; you may be sure that he will not want to leave it, nor will you wish him to do so. At the same time, it is imperative that he stay within gun range. The approved procedure is to stop the dog within the proper limits, either with the whistle signal or voice command, whichever you prefer to use. When you have come up with the spaniel, he can again be cast on the line of scent. With a racing ringneck, it may be necessary to halt the dog several times until the pheasant is finally overtaken and flushed within shooting range. Also, if you hunt a Retriever in spaniel fashion, this same procedure is employed.

In the case of setters and pointers that are expected to range quite independently with "bird sense," the trainer may wish to school the dog in systematic ranging merely as added control in the field and to be of assistance when searching for single birds of a scattered bevy. Actually, professional handlers engaged in the development of pointing dogs for field trials are no longer concerned with inculcation of the quartering lesson as in days gone by. These handlers are, from the very first, looking for "running" dogs, ambitious rangers, and efforts are directed toward only satisfactory field trial handling response from the dog. Most of the modern professionals have a retinue of assistants and the service of a scout in actual competition on the major circuit; this has given rise to the spectacular range witnessed in the leading trials, a single exception being the National Championship at Grand Junction, Tennessee, where subservience to the gun is still a rigid requirement. The fact that handlers are seldom called to work their dogs on a scattered bevy in field trials has also played a part in the abandonment of the quartering lessons. Of course, if the character and temperament and tendencies of the individual dog warrant such instruction, or it is a means to an end, the present-day professional will utilize methods similar to those explained.

The principal purpose of quartering lessons for the gun dog is so that in the shooting field the particular coverts to be hunted may be selected and worked in preferred sequence. Incidentally, with the top flight grouse trial dogs, in Pennsylvania, Michigan, and the New England states, the approved quartering standard seems to be a natural inclination or tendency, for in the brush it never requires much tutelage to get the quality grouse dog to range correctly.

In educating pointing dogs to quarter, one can use the check cord as explained in connection with spaniels in order to familiarize the dog with the whistle signal and what it signifies. But when out for the actual lesson in ranging, select a field quite clear of obstructions, preferably a forty or fifty acre plot, rectangular in shape and fenced. You start to walk up the center of the field, casting the dog first to the right, taking a few steps in that direction yourself, then when the dog nears the fence or the termination of his cast, which is likely to end before the boundary is reached, be alert to sound the note on your whistle, motion with your arm (or with hat in hand) to the dog as you start toward the opposite side of the field. The dog will hustle to get ahead of you; permit him to go on to the fence, if he will, then repeat with the whistle, motion again and change your direction. Try to anticipate the dog; just as his cast ends and he is due to turn, or an instant before, blow your whistle. Always work into the wind, because this will influence the dog to make his turns in the proper direction. You will take a restricted zigzag course up the field, the dog making similar but wider swings. Do not make these lessons long. If your pupil doesn't seem to get even a vague idea of what you are attempting out of the first few trys, do not be discouraged. Repetition will bring success. But keep the lessons short; sustain your dog's keenness with suitable diversion or rest in between each session. A ten-minute lesson should be followed by a quarter hour recess. If your pupil shows signs of fatigue, stop at once.

Your dog should know well the meaning of "Whoa." If in the course of quartering he attempts to cross behind you, do not permit it. Or if he persists in turning with an inside loop, set about to correct this. It can be accomplished by stopping the dog in his tracks with uplifted arm and the command, "Whoa," when he is coming in toward you from the right hand side, then signal him with a wave of your arm in the direction you desire him to turn. If he does not turn properly, call him to you, but stop him en route, then go to him, take hold of his collar, force him to turn correctly and send him back to the right side of the field with an outward turn. Get him well accustomed to this particular turn, then follow a similar method when he is approaching you from the left. By proceeding up the field at good pace afoot, or by giving this lesson while mounted on horseback, the trainer will incite the dog to turn outward which the canine may do quite automatically so that he will be keeping in front.

When you take the dog to an environment more likely to hold game than the first relatively bare field used, you will be able to direct him to the cover you wish searched, but do not permit any loitering or pottering on the part of the dog. Urge him, if the need arises, to keen and lively hunting.

Of course, the perfection of these lessons will be evidenced as your dog will make a barely perceptible pause for direction at the whistle, in the same instant casting in the direction of your own movement accompanied by an arm gesture. In fact, response will be developed to such a superlative degree that at the signal to turn the dog without slackening stride will, apparently intuitively, bend around properly.

When the pointer or setter is searching birdy country, he is expected to confine his hunting to promising cover. His casts should be intelligently directed to tempting objectives and the dog should not be expected to cross a bare field merely to get on the other side of the handler, but ought to range forward to what appears to be productive coverts and hunt this on his way to the opposite side. In the classic words of Snuffy Smith, "time's a-wasting" if the hunting dog does not make every step count in the search for game.

It is important to caution against over-handling. Allow the dog to exercise his own initiative so far as possible, do not hack him, refrain from unnecessary commands, constant coaching, and undue fretting. Have confidence in your dog to do the job right. It is surprising how a shaky handler, fearful of his dog making a mistake, seems to prompt the very error he is worrying about. It might be well to say a few words about telepathic communication between master and dog in the next chapter.

CHAPTER XVII

Telepathic Communication Between Trainer and Dog

Is there telepathy between the trainer and his dog? Does the latter respond to the moods, the fears, the uncertainties of the former? And does the confidence of the trainer inspire a similar feeling in the dog? These questions might open up a very broad field of discussion. It is a psychological fact that such influences exist among human beings, and from careful observation of various occurrences with hunting dogs in the shooting field and at field trials, it is inescapable that there is thought transference between master and dog.

Telepathy, according to the dictionary, is apparent communication from one mind to another otherwise than through the channels of sense. We have always held a firm belief in the theory that the subconscious expression of the trainer's personality is reflected and manifested in the actions of his dog. This is seen so frequently that there can be no doubt of it. Close study of the work of various professional trainers over a period of years enables one to tell almost invariably what particular breaker has been responsible for a dog's early education, even though the dog may be in new hands at the time. This is possible because of the identifying peculiarities the dog displays in his work. Every handler has his own system. True, a great many may follow similar methods in the development and training of dogs in their charge, but each has some little individual characteristic which is reflected in the dog. Some trainers may believe in constant coaching by voice, and a dog so educated comes to depend upon this coaching; placed in new hands, he will not work in his customary manner unless a similar technique is employed by the handler, or sufficient work must ensue before the dog adjusts himself and his performance to the different tactics of the educator who works quietly. And isn't this a logical place to interpolate that when one has a dog trained by a professional handler, it is essential that the owner familiarize himself with the handling methods of the trainer and use the same commands so that the dog will not be confused when at work?

Every experienced professional handler could recite numerous instances of telepathic communication between himself and his dog.

A Pointer displays style and intensity

How he has seemingly conveyed his desires to the dog by thought transference without an outward sign or spoken command. He could relate incidents of inspiring confidence in a not completely trained dog and how the dog came through with flying colors. Conversely, how he began to worry about an old reliable dog and that this lack of trust seemingly betrayed the dog into error.

Amazing examples could be included here of how a trainer of proved competency lost confidence in a dog's ability and thereafter could make little or no headway with that particular prospect, whereas another, perhaps an amateur lacking the experience and skill of the other trainer, but with implicit confidence in the dog's ability to do it right, could have the pupil perform perfectly. We could also describe cases where a dog which was capable of perfect performance while being handled by his original trainer, when placed in the hands of another professional could not approach the former excellence of his work.

We have witnessed many instances in field trial competition where the unwavering faith a handler reposed in his dog was repaid in the dog's super performance. Not only in pointing dog trials, but in spaniel events and Retriever competitions. This matter of confidence is strongly reflected when a dog is called upon to back the point of a bracemate. The handler who brings his dog in quietly and lets him have his head, evidencing assurance that the dog will honor at sight, generally is rewarded by seeing his dog back properly without a word of caution. On the other hand, a handler who displays considerable trepidation that his dog will not back and proceeds to coach and caution nervously is in large measure responsible for the fact that his dog invariably neglects to honor correctly. It is not the intention of the writer to enumerate a number of specific instances, but reference will be made to the case of the celebrated pointer, Seaview Rex, and his able handler, R. D. (Bobby) Bevan.

Field trial fans count both Seaview Rex and Bobby Bevan as familiars. The two won a large measure of fame in leading quail trials and veteran followers of the bird dog sport can tell you of Seaview Rex's invincibility on the grounds of the old United States Club at Grand Junction, Tenn., while on the other side of that little southern community, on the historic Ames Plantation over which the National Championship is run, Rex never did perform as phenomenally as he did on the U. S. grounds. True, in two renewals of the classic National Championship, Rex was accorded the newspaper distinction of runner-up laurels; that was in 1926 and 1928, when the setter, Feagin's Mohawk Pal, won the title both times. But several times Seaview Rex was an odds-on favorite, in a manner of speaking, but never did capture this crown.

We recall one year when Rex was a top-heavy favorite at the time of the drawing for the National Championship. Bob Bevan had brought him to Grand Junction during the last week in December that winter, full of confidence that he had his dog just right and when Rex was put down in the Amateur Quail Championship, the first of the long series of trials at Grand Junction, he

was unquestionably in the finest of form and as perfect in his manner on game and in handling as one could desire. The dog won
that two-hour race in a brilliant heat; indeed, it was one of the best
performances witnessed during the entire series at Grand Junction.
The next week Rex started in the All-America trials under different
judges and won the All-Age Stake just as easily. Next came the
United States All-Age Stake. Here, under still another set of judges,
he won again. Thus, in three weeks the dog had won three first

Brittany Spaniel with pheasant

places and loomed up as a most formidable candidate for the National Championship.

What happened? There were twenty dogs in the classic event and
Seaview Rex was drawn to run with Rod M as the very last brace
of the lot. As the National Championship heats are three hours in
length only four dogs can be run in a day, consequently the Seaview Rex-Rod M heat was not scheduled to take place until Friday
afternoon. If the reader has ever observed a handler waiting day
after day to run his dog, hearing the reports every evening, he may
readily imagine what a severe tension is created. During this interval
of weary waiting, to make matters worse, Bevan took a severe cold

which laid him up for several days and thus physical disability augmented his mental state.

This watching and waiting around a field trial, in anticipation of the day to run a dog, is indubitably one of the most nerve-racking experiences a professional trainer—or amateur handler, for that matter—is called upon to undergo. Bob Bevan frankly admitted that his nerves were shot to pieces during that period of waiting and the nearer it came to the time of running his dog, the more dubious he felt—and yet all that week the reports came in from the field that nothing brilliant had been seen and that it was anybody's race.

Noon came on Friday. All the dogs had been run but the two Every disinterested observer was frank enough to admit that while not a scintillating race had been seen, that of Becky Broom Hill was about the best, though it was far from being unbeatable. But Bob Bevan, as he himself admitted, was on the verge of stage fright when he led Rex out that afternoon. The casual follower in the gallery might not have been aware of this, but those who knew Bob Bevan well, and had seen him pilot on numerous occasions before, sensed the situation. It is a well known truism that fear takes the punch out of everything that he who is suffering from it does. Was this stage fright communicated to Seaview Rex? Whether this was really the case or not is a problem, but the fact remains that Rex did not get away with the boldness and cocksureness which marked his earlier exhibitions. Those who had never seen Rex run before probably did not notice this, nor did they realize that Bob Bevan had also lost much of his usual equanimity. Before the first hour was up, it was apparent to all who knew handler and dog, that they were battling in a lost cause. Bevan and Rex worked in unison, no doubt, but it was only twenty-five per cent normal and the cause was lost before the lead was ever taken off of Seaview Rex's neck.

Most all trainers experience these situations at some time in their career, especially under circumstances such as these. It is not a new thing and many instances of a similar kind could be related. That is why the veteran professional will tell you unequivocally that the hunting dog knows what you're thinking about and that your emotions are transmitted to him.

We remember one time in a Retriever trial, where a dog had been sent on a blind, difficult retrieve, and he had taken directions from his handler in superb style. But as he neared the mark, the wind was wrong, and that handler literally leaned like the Tower of Pisa in the effort to bend his dog to gain full advantage of the wind when he reached the location where the game had been marked. Was it telepathy—or the balancing act the handler put on—which prompted the dog to angle exactly right to make a quick find and perfect retrieve?

Watch a handler carefully, study his emotions as expressed by his demeanor and actions, and then remark the amazing way in which dogs frequently respond to such stimulus or inspiration without any conventional signals or directions. Telepathy certainly has to be considered in the training of dogs and in the actual performance of dogs in the hunting field. The canine pupil indubitably reacts to the mood of his instructor.

CHAPTER XVIII

The Pointing Instinct

The instincts of pure-bred sporting dogs are the expression of ancestral action handed down by heredity. Dogs of these breeds have well defined hunting propensities as hereditary characteristics. In the case of pointing dogs, it is instinctive to indicate the presence of game by pointing—standing motionless facing the scent to show the location of the birds. With these dogs the tendency is a natural predisposition strengthened by years of selective breeding. This is not to say that the inclination to point is an exclusive heritage of only a few breeds—the tendency to pause before springing upon prey is manifested by many animals.

All successful trainers of bird dogs have made a study of the various manifestations of the pointing instinct and it goes without saying that a dilettante who undertakes the education of his dog should know something about this trait in order to develop it properly. So even at the risk of including material with which most of our readers are familiar, a discussion of the subject is undertaken.

It is beyond dispute that the pointing instinct is peculiarly intense in pointers and setters and that steadiness on game can be taught these varieties much more readily than other breeds, but it must not be supposed that this outstanding trait of the bird dog was implanted within him solely for the benefit of man, nor that it is impossible to cultivate it in other canine species. It is simply typical of the dog's wild ancestors, adapted and perfected in pointing dogs to the use of man, through generations of breeding, habit, and training. Many writers have described the statuesque point of the bird dog as a cataleptic condition which transpires when he encounters the scent of game and that it is involuntary and akin to mesmeric influence. The phenomenon, as a matter of fact, is neither cataleptic nor mesmeric. It is simply suddenly suspended motion as an act of precaution on striking scent, which the dog's wild ancestors employed in capturing small prey. This *pause before springing* is also a characteristic of other wild animals.

In the case of the bird dog, hunters discovered that they could put this characteristic to their own use and thus began to develop

"Like Father, Like Son." Sire and Son pointing quail in Texas. Father, right and in front. Son only 16 months old

the pointing dog, coaching him to remain in that position and not touch the prey, which was in reality his own by right of discovery, while the master did the killing for him—or rather for himself. Be it as it may, the dog was a party to the killing and thus his interest was maintained.

Training for generation after generation after generation has confirmed the trait until now the character is inherited in our bird dogs with the degree of certainty of all other inherited characteristics.

The dog upon striking scent is in full possession of his faculties; his eyes may dilate, his jaws open and close, his muscles twitch. The intoxicating odor tells him that prey is just ahead and all the primitive qualities of his ancestors come into play and only the training of generations of ancestors and his own schooling hold him so he submits to his master doing the killing, while he plays second fiddle.

The young dog will frequently make a point as stylish and even more intense when he comes upon his game than the aged campaigner, but being untrained and therefore knowing no restraint, it will likely be of the "flash" variety, which means the dog will quickly jump in, flush and chase, and the more of this he does the keener will become his desire to find game and so accentuates the passion for hunting. The pupil possessing this overwhelming emotion is a most promising one, for the dog which has no desire to seek for game isn't worth a nickel and it is a waste of time to endeavor to educate him. What good is it to teach him to fetch and carry to drop, to come in and all the other attainments of the finished shooting dog, if the primary instinct of hunting is lacking? Having a puppy which possesses this instinct to a high degree, the trainer must know when to steady him on his game. That is the crucial time in the bird dog's life and the most delicate period in his training, for it is at this time more dogs are made or marred than at any other. It is then that "blinkers" are created. The handler must use due caution and treat each pupil which comes to him for training as an entity. Some dogs develop steadiness with little cautioning or correction; others require more time. What may be quite right for one puppy is ruination to another. The teacher at this stage must know how to govern himself as well as the pupil. The calm, level-headed man who constantly controls his temper may bring a dog through this crucial phase and have him steady on his game without taking one whit of the admirable quality from the puppy, while a less adept person might make a slow, mechanical, pottering dog out of the same animal, and still another wreck him entirely.

To make a good pointing dog out of a promising youngster without robbing him of his individuality, his dash or his boldness and character, requires close study and extreme care. The best trainers will sometimes go wrong, and occasionally the poorest tutor will have success, dependent largely upon what kind of material each has to work with. But striking an average, the clever man who studies his subjects as individuals and is able to bring them along according to each one's talents, will enjoy the finest fruits of success.

Experienced trainers assert that the pointing instinct is not, as it seems, a single impulse, but is made up of a number of minor instincts, each of which operates so that the resultant action is the manifestation we term pointing. The act by the dog may be likened to a piece of machinery—an automobile motor, say. There are many parts that must co-ordinate before the machine as a whole will func-

Pointer on Game

tion. The more perfect the construction, the more readily will each part do its work.

So, too, with the pointing instinct. Each little element has a duty to perform and these must all work at once; should some laggard lesser urge fail momentarily to "spark," the excellence of the ultimate point is marred.

The dog's delicate nose informs him that game is near; the will to stop asserts itself; all the mystical senses that go to make the point respond! Once the nose apprehends the scent of nearby game, it will not do for either the psychical or physical parts to lag; the performance of each must be instantaneous, so prompt in fact that what we see is the single action—the point!

If the sportsman follows public field trials, he will witness a great variety of points. When we see a dog going at a lively clip, then suddenly whirl and snap into a lofty stand, head held high and tail up, we call it a stylish point. Some dogs do not trouble to "make game," that is, indicate the proximity of birds by so-called feathering. With breath-taking suddenness these just seem to jump into a thrilling attitude—and that is the type we most favor. There are other dogs which become busily engaged when they approach close to game, feather enthusiastically while locating it accurately, then point positively—and the attractiveness of the final pose is admirable.

There are still other dogs which require considerable time before establishing their point and then strike an indifferent, if not sloppy, attitude. One may also encounter a type that seems to try earnestly, but whose points are not attractive. They appear to get a wee bit of their pointing constitution in action at once, but other parts come along phlegmatically. Some dogs are physically imperfect for the making of a good point. Dogs with angulated shoulders and legs set far under them cannot stop at the instantaneous command of the will; carried a step too far by their momentum, this step is often fatal. The psychical machinery may start in time, but the physical construction results in sluggish action.

The type of dog which possesses all the parts necessary to make a perfect point, but for some unaccountable reason seems slow getting into action, generally will evidence considerable improvement if he is given opportunity to get all his minor instincts in the habit of working together smoothly. Seasoned handlers with dogs of this kind do not hesitate to allow them to jump into their points, even at the risk of a flush, for this will promote co-ordination and develop the kind of performer we all like to see.

The exact moment a dog will establish his first definite point on wild game cannot be forecast precisely. Some dogs of the pointing breeds have an overwhelming desire to point and do so at an early age and frequently with but little incentive. Others may not come to pointing until they are many months old.

A dog can be taught to point by what is termed artificial means. This method is to place a bird in a certain spot, lead the dog up to it so that he may catch the scent and if he does not point it spontaneously, check him into a point. Such stands are of the "Whoa" variety. We do not approve this technique because the normal, instinctive action of the dog is preferable, and the dogs with such natural quality are most valuable for breeding purposes. Since we have little patience with the "Whup" point, no space will be used to describe how a dog can be educated by artificial means, whether by sight or scent, whether indoors or out.

The best method for training is to await the dog's natural manifestation of the pointing instinct. Just when this will be, no one can say definitely. We remember talking with the scholarly Charles H. Babcock, developer and handler of Manitoba Rap, first pointer to ever win the National Championship, of John Proctor, winner of four outstanding titles, and numerous other celebrated performers. Let it be added that both Manitoba Rap and John Proctor were extraordinarily prepotent as sires. Asked for his opinion about the time a puppy should be finished, Babcock replied:

"Diligent, careful work every day on the prairies, giving the puppy a good time with plenty of opportunity on game, with no cares or worries for the dog or for me, yet asking him that question daily, and some fine morning when the weather's cool, the dew upon the grass, the dog bending every energy to find his game, he will answer and I'll know that he's telling me the truth. As plainly as human speech could tell it, I'll know that he has sowed his wild oats, shed his puppy ways and is ready for his mission in life.

"While it is perfectly all right to begin training as early as possible, due care and judgment must be used as to the proper time to finish the dog. Fear has nothing in common with the desire to find birds. Perhaps a dog will when he is young, stand the gaff and the hurry. He is impetuous and will continue to hunt regardless of the penalty inflicted for flushing. Later he gets wise and is not so anxious to find game, not so stylish when he has found it. You can never know how much a dog will stand until you have spoiled him, and it is then too late."

The remarks of Charley Babcock may well serve as a warning, like the bell at a railroad crossing to the motorist. Let the dog come to pointing his game without being crowded, as a natural development of his heritage, and then proceed with care so that his usefulness will not be impaired or the brilliance of his performance dulled.

CHAPTER XIX

Steadiness on Point

Your bird dog, in the course of his advancement, has been given planned outings in the field and his zest for hunting has increased so that he displays a veritable passion for searching out and finding birds, an occasional flash point preceding a vigorous chase. Meanwhile, the various lessons in yard training have resulted in perfect obedience to the different commands. The educator is now alert to determine the psychological time for finishing the dog, making him stanch on point, also steady to wing and shot.

As explained by the late C. H. Babcock, who was quoted in the preceding chapter, the day will come when the dog shall establish a point and hold it sufficiently long for the handler to reach his side. From then on, nothing will be gained by letting the dog chase, unless the handler does this for a definite reason, as mentioned in the description of the technique employed by the veteran Jake Bishop.

When the dog has given evidence of prolonging his flash points, the astute handler will endeavor to set the scene to help in this lesson. He will take the dog afield under favorable circumstances, when scenting conditions are excellent and when he knows where in suitable cover a bevy of quail may likely be found. He casts the dog off in such a way that when the dog approaches the habitat of the game, he will have the wind in his nose and in his favor every factor that might be of assistance in the establishment of a point. Under normal circumstances, such care will be rewarded. But if the dog does not hold a point until he can be reached, the educator must "set the stage" again.

There are those who adopt the technique of working a dog until he is tired enough to prolong his point rather than dash in, flush, and chase. We do not recommend this procedure. For one thing, fatigue in a hunting dog prompts pottering. You will take less from your dog if you have him keen, full of fire and energy, and there

Photo by W. Eugene Smith

Note check cord on Setter. Handler is giving the lesson in stanchness on point and steadiness to flush

will be no extra work entailed if you plan carefully. Besides the dog undoubtedly will display a great deal more style and character on his point while he is fresh and bubbling over with vigor. There are dogs which are real stylists on point when strong and lively, but which as their energies become exhausted lose much of their loftiness and character on game.

Style and intensity on point are always admired by the shooter as well as the field trial patron, and the various degrees shown by different dogs are discussed frequently. Character should broadly be interpreted to mean that phase of a dog's work on game which includes intensity and positiveness. The dog which slinks up on his game with lowered tail and an uncertain attitude cannot be credited with much charm, while, on the other hand, the dog that is sure of purpose is brimful of not only character, but individuality and decision. Picturesque pointing attitudes are not at all unusual with dogs of this caliber, and incisive work on game produces even greater thrills than filling the game bag!

We come to the time when the dog establishes a pretty point and the educator encourages him to stanchness with a reassuring "Whoa." The trainer approaches the dog cautiously in order to avoid exciting the dog's temptation to break in and flush the game, preferably coming from the side and around in front rather than from directly behind the dog. As the dog stands on point, snap the check cord to his collar if he has not been dragging it, caution "Whoa," a command with which the dog is fully familiar. The dog may be quivering like an aspen leaf, but he is to be reassured by you in the most soothing tones and a hand signal confirms him in his position. It is not well to prolong this first point unduly because the game may retire to a considerable distance afoot or even escape entirely. Now the dog is warned "Whoa," the birds are flushed and, if the dog attempts to break in, he is halted with the check cord, returned to the spot where he has been pointing, commanded "Whoa," and made to remain there, while the handler walks about, even going a little distance away, but under no circumstances is the dog permitted to move. In the event that he does, he is to be replaced at once. The order, "Whoa," is repeated, and "Steady" may be added.

Proper use of the check cord will hasten the steadying of the dog. Two methods are suggested: (a) With the assistance of a helper, see that the cord is held taut to keep the dog in position when the birds are flushed and the shot fired; (b) Allow the dog to break in and chase, and when the dog in hot pursuit has reached the limit of the check cord, up-end him with a firm grasp on your end of the cord by throwing your weight opposite to the dog's direction.

Er Shelley, distinguished author of "Twentieth Century Bird Dog Training," advocates permitting the dog to break to the end of a long check line, then turn him in backward somersault fashion. Shelley insists that he has never known a dog to run into the end of the cord and an abrupt up-ending more than three times. This, unquestionably, is a most effective method because the shock sustained by the dog is something that stays in his memory, yet the experience is not overly drastic.

If an assistant is available, it is sufficient to hold the dog in his pointing position by use of taut check cord, accompanied by the command for steadiness.

Because of the undeniable importance of this critical phase of the bird dog's education, we strongly recommend that if it is at all possible the services of an experienced assistant be enlisted; if you have a helper, you can devote your entire attention to the dog, holding him steady with the cord, and your assistant can kill a bird for your pupil. At the outset, steady the dog to wing only; do not fire over these first points and even resign yourself to forfeiting some later opportunities to kill game while the dog's education is uncompleted.

After the dog fully understands what is expected of him in the way of steadiness to flush of game and to shot, the check cord can be discarded. Its elimination may prompt the dog to break. Go after him and bring him back to the spot. If he gets out of hand, do not chase after him, shouting commands; merely mark the spot with your hat or other object, then await your opportunity to peaceably lead or forcibly haul the dog back, chide him for this lack of obedience and require him to remain in position while you walk around the place.

Do not punish the impetuous dog unless you are certain he clearly associates the punishment with the error he has committed. Let us re-emphasize that care must be exercised to avoid making the dog shy of game. Injudicious handling of the dog at this period might result in his developing into a "blinker," a dog that purposely, in one form or another, evades pointing game. Hence, you should have a clear understanding of your dog's temperament before this part of his education is undertaken. If he is strong-willed, overly bold, and independent, you may use harsh commands and enforce obedience once he has understood what is wanted. On the other hand, with a shy, timid pupil, encouragement rather than restraint may be in order.

When the dog will point stanchly and hold until you reach him, there is no great trick to securing his steadiness to wing and to

Photo by W. Eugene Smith

Confirming "stanchness" on point

shot. While he is on point, the trainer should go to him and place his hands upon the dog, the left hand in front of the dog's chest (not a bad precaution), then stroke him gently with the right hand along his back to the base of the tail. Do not hesitate to handle the dog on point. This will have a beneficial effect in making him stanch. The trainer will also apply light pressure from the rear in an apparent effort to force the dog ahead into the birds; the dog will undoubtedly brace himself to resist. Of course, the attempt will not be so strong as to force the dog off his feet. It is permissible, even advisable, in many cases for the handler to lift the

Photo by W. Eugene Smith

While the dog points stanchly, the handler drops the check cord and advances to flush the birds

dog off the ground, then replace him unceremoniously, stroke his tail and hold it at a stylish angle. Insist upon steadiness to wing and shot under all circumstances and, when the time is ripe, drop a bird so that the dog may see the fall, then encourage him to retrieve it.

Do not think that your dog will never break and chase again. There may be lapses. Your canine comrade is not an automaton without emotions. The fact is that at the least expected moment, the dog in an overexuberance of spirits may act like an unschooled puppy. The experienced trainer tries to anticipate any fall from grace on the part of an impetuous pupil, and thus more quickly gains that reliability of finished performance that characterizes the work of the veteran campaigner.

When the dog has become quite reliable in his pointing, it is time for the breaker to begin to approach him from various angles, to make sundry noises and motions which may make the dog nervous at first, but to which he must be accustomed so that it will not

J. Horace Lytle prepares to flush in front of a point by his Setter, Sam Illsley

disturb him on point. The dog should display unconcerned stanchness to shouting, whistling, shooting, so even reverberations of a galloping field trial gallery will not disquiet him or make him break his point. Of course, it has been taken for granted that the trainer will voice proper words of praise for the dog when he performs well.

The behavior of a dog on game, both before and after the birds are flushed, as well as the style displayed on point, reveal to a marked extent the character and skill of the trainer and the methods that have been employed in training. There are dogs which, as soon as their handler approaches to flush the birds, will drop or slink to one side, as if they were expecting to be punished. In other cases, a complete letdown, a loss of all snap and vitality, is noticeable at the approach of the handler. This evidence of fear is in some cases the result of severe chastisement for flushing, breaking shot, or chasing. In other instances it can be attributed to an overly sensitive nervous organization. In any event, careful study of the individual dog should be made before additional educational measures are decided upon.

There have been notable examples cited of famous setters and pointers and the means of training them. Ivo H. Regenold, a brother-in-law of the celebrated professional handler, Dave Rose, served as assistant to "Uncle Dave" for many years, being with him in the days of Tony Boy, Wun Lung and other great setters of that period, and here is Regenold's classic description of the breaking of Tony Boy. Ivo said:

"That dog sho' was the hardest proposition I ever did see, but we finally got him right. Mr. Rose often felt like givin' it up, though, as a bad job. I don't guess that you could handle many dogs like we did Tony Boy, but with him it worked all right, and by the time of the United States Derby in January, with Tony Boy twenty months old, he was pointin' and holdin' his birds like an All-Age dog.

"It's a long time ago, but I remember Tony jist as well as if I had him yesterday," he continued. "He was the goin'est dog I ever did see, but he sho' had a head of his own. Tony Boy made his first start in the Derby of the Manitoba Trials in September, 1894, where he won third, but it wasn't his bird work that won him that place, for at that time he'd chase all the birds out of the country. He was some puppy, though, and everybody said if he ever could be broke he'd make a great dog. I always liked Tony, but Mr. Rose never would let me handle him. Tony came back from the prairies and was the same headstrong dog and chased quail jist like he did chickens. He was started in the trials that were held that year in North Caroliny and got a place there in the setter Derby, second. After that Mr. Rose brought him to Lawrenceburg, Tennessee, and he says: 'Ivy, we've got to break Tony so he'll hold his birds, and we must do it before the January trials.' And I said, 'All right, Mr. Rose; I guess if anybody kin break him, we kin.' We had a lot of birds on the preserve there and so it was no trouble in givin' him plenty of chances. There was a big bevy jist about a hundred yards from the house and every time we turned Tony loose he'd make a dash for that bevy, pop 'em up and then go chasin' after the singles until he had 'em all chased out of the country. No whistlin' or callin' or anything else would do the least bit of good. Tony'd just go after them till he was good and ready to come in, and then he'd come, but not before.

"One mawnin' Mr. Rose came out to the kennels, where I was cleanin' up, with a 25 foot cord in his hand, and says, 'Ivy, we're goin' to break Tony this mawnin',' and I says, 'All right, Mr. Rose.' 'I'm goin' to put this check cord on him,' says he, 'and I want you to go down by the branch where that bevy stays and hide. When he pops 'em, you grab the rope and pull back good and hard and every time you pull him back give him a cut and call him by name.'

"Mr. Rose started the dog out in the other direction, 'cause he knowed he'd swing around anyway and get that bevy. I wasn't there long until I heerd Tony comin' through the cover, lickety click, lickety click, with the rope swishin' through the weeds behind him. Afore I knowed it, pop! goes the birds, and I makes a dash for the rope and misses it, but I fell into the ditch all right. But I was up and after him right away. Tony went right down the branch were the scattered birds settled and, pop! out goes one. Then he puts up another, but by that time I was close behind him and jist as he popped the third one I fell down on the rope and give it such a yank that Tony turned clean over.

"Old Tony acted mighty lak' he was s'prised that someone could ketch him so easy, but I done give him a good dressin', as Mr. Rose told me to do, and I called him by name with every lick I give him. Mr. Rose came up about then and we turned him loose once more. He only went a few yards and pointed jist as nice as anyone wants to see. I grabbed the rope again, but he was steady and when Mr. Rose killed the bird fur him old Tony acted lak' it was an everyday occurrence fur him to point. Did ye ever see Tony point?" he asked. "Well, if you did, you know there wasn't another dog that pointed with the style and fire he had. He sho' was a picture."

"Did that one experience break him?" was asked.

"Oh, no sah," said Regenold. "We give him the same workout every mawnin' and he popped 'em a couple of times more, but I got him jist as he popped a bevy, and after that he was a broke dog. Mr. Rose took him to the United States trials at West Point, Mississippi, and he won second in the best field of setter puppies ever out. Tony's Gale beat him, but the next week he won the Southern Derby, where he beat the same dogs. Tony's Gale was second there and the pointer, Delhi, was third. But Mr. Rose was always sho' of Tony Boy after we give him that workin' over on the old trainin' grounds at Lawrenceburg, and I want to tell you Mr. Rose had a lot o' good dogs, but Tony Boy was the captain of 'em all."

CHAPTER XX

Stopping to Flush or Shot

As soon as the dog points stanchly and exhibits steadiness to wing and under the gun, the trainer will teach him to stop to the flight of game, whether the flush is accidental or deliberate. Professional field trial handlers debate the desirability of having the dog stop to flush. For example, in field trial competition a dog may top a rise and out of sight of everyone inadvertently lift a bevy of quail, but if true to his training he stops promptly and remains motionless in a pointing position, when his handler and the judges ride over the crest, point will be called for the dog. When the handler rides up, the attitude of the dog may indicate clearly to him that the game has flown, nevertheless on the judicial score sheet an unproductive point is likely to be chalked against the dog. Now if Rap or Count had not been trained to stop to flush, such a charge never would be scored against him under those circumstances.

On the other hand, where a dog stops promptly to flush in view of his handler, the alert pilot will call "Point," quickly adding, "There go the birds," and if the judges were not looking at the dog when this transpired, he may receive credit for a point where the bevy flushed wild. In any event, unless the flush is noted as a deliberate one, judges will not discredit the dog, but rather consider the action as evidence of the excellence of his training.

For ordinary gunning purposes, all hunting dogs should be trained to stop to flush and at the sound of the gun. This is most desirable in the pointing breeds, and absolutely essential for spaniels and Retrievers. The methods to be employed have been described in connection with previous training lessons, so it should suffice to touch briefly upon the approved technique.

Every time the dog is responsible for the flush of game, command "Whoa" and require him to halt in the exact place where he was when the game took wing. It will indubitably be necessary in such circumstances to go after him and bring him back to the spot several times. Greatest caution should be exercised so that this will not dull the dog's enthusiasm. After he understands what is required of him, application of some force should result in gratifying obedience. The chances are your dog will be the cause of flushing more

Preparing to confirm stanchness on point; availability of check cord will aid in making dog steady to flush

game than he may point at the outset, especially if he is worked among scattered birds, but this will gain him valuable experience that shall serve him in good stead.

After you have trained the dog so that he will stop immediately when he causes a flush, you can perfect him so that the whir of wings as game birds boil from cover will be sufficient to halt him in his tracks.

Stopping to shot in the field is an extension of yard training. When the dog is ranging freely but not at a great distance, the educator fires a shot and at the detonation commands the dog, "Whoa." If the yard training has been thoroughly absorbed, immediate obedience on the part of the dog is given. If the dog does not halt instantly, the handler must take him right back to the spot where he was when the shot sounded and the order was given. This lesson is repeated until the dog understands that he must stop at the sound of the gun whether or not a spoken order accompanies it.

It is strongly advised that while teaching the dog steadiness to wing and exacting obedience so that he stops to flush or shot, the canine pupil not be called upon to do any retrieving, even though birds may be killed over some of these points. Later, it will be easy to apply the retrieving lessons to assure greater usefulness of the dog in the hunting field.

Breaking shot is a bad habit, principally caused by over-anxiety on the part of the dog, or lack of training, which is to say that the primary instincts of the dog have not been properly subjugated. There is another cause, one that lies entirely with the instructor. Over-eagerness on the part of the hunter may be the reason the dog breaks, for with the drop of the bird some gunners want to rush directly to the spot and it goes without saying what the effect on the dog is bound to be. Be steady yourself and you will help dissuade any inclination on the part of the dog to break shot. It is good practice not to send a dog in too quickly to hunt dead and retrieve, for if this is done immediately after firing, it emboldens a tendency to break in at once.

There may be an occasion where your usually reliable gun dog suddenly bolts in at shot. Do not be too quick to charge him with a fault; a dog intuitively seems to know when a bird is crippled and under certain conditions a quick dash to the "fall" may be an exhibition of remarkable intelligence on the part of the dog, and certainly nothing for which he should be reprimanded. This is just another instance where the trainer is expected to be master of the situation at all times and analyze the work quickly, accurately. Certainly the order of intelligence should at least be on a parity with that displayed by the dog.

The *experienced* dog should also be permitted to exercise his own judgment in respect to marking where the scattered birds from a bevy have pitched, or in searching the area of the "fall" of dead or wounded game. Many times the faculty of a dog for marking transcends that of the human hunter. In interpretation of such work some latitude must be allowed the well trained and experienced dog. If his efforts on his own initiative do not get results, he will respond to your orders and you can then direct him as you desire. Such a policy should not be adopted with the green, inexperienced dog, but do not be too quick to condemn a usually reliable performer for a mistake in judgment.

It is an old saying that the real judge of good bird dog performance would rather see a classy flush than a slovenly, inde-

"Whoa, Steady"

cisive point. The manner in which a dog establishes his points can be directed to a certain extent by the trainer. It is of utmost significance that the dog be taught to point only body scent and locate his game with unerring accuracy. If the handler insists on abnormal care on the part of the dog, the odds are in favor of developing a grass prowler that will point just as soon as he encounters any scent whatsoever. This makes for pottering, pointing of foot scent, trailing laboriously with low head—in short, anything but the incisive, snappy, thrilling performance that is the hallmark of the class bird dog.

When teaching steadiness to wing and shot, the trainer is warned therefore to be careful of too much coaching or cautioning of his dog. When the dog has had sufficient experience to distinguish between various emanations, whether body scent, foot scent or from a roost, he should be schooled in pointing stanchly only when you feel certain he has the body effluvia strong in his nostrils. The schooling consists principally of self-restraint on the part of the educator. The dog is not to be encouraged to point foot scent; when his experience enables him to discriminate between scents, he should be permitted to work out any scent situations in his own way, for the more of these perplexing problems he solves, the greater will be his value as a bird dog.

As a rule, a dog will point when he encounters a hot foot scent; a moment or so later he will display a tendency to move on. This is the instant the trainer should refrain from an impulse to check the dog with "Whoa." Of course, one may think he is anticipating a desire on the part of the dog to move up and flush the game, but at this stage of the dog's development the handler need not worry unduly about that. If the breaker by voice or signal forces the dog to hold a point on foot scent when the dog's own judgment is to advance until he possesses the body effluvia, the dog's development in the proper direction is retarded. Pursuit of such a course will in time habituate the dog to point stanchly when all he has is foot scent.

There are different ways dogs will locate birds after encountering foot scent. One dog may road along in the wake of the birds, aided by the trail of scent, advancing until he has the body emanations properly. Just so long as he doesn't nose the ground, such work is acceptable. Another dog will toss his head high and, discerning the body scent, draw directly to the location of the birds, marching forward like a drum majorette. Still another, pausing to determine the direction in which the birds traveled, breaks away from the trail entirely, then quarters the cover with the advantage of the wind until he nails the bevy accurately.

The tendency to locate body scent in a particular way is more or less a natural inclination with individual dogs, and the breaker cannot do a great deal about it. But he can avert the dog dwelling on foot scent. When the pupil falters or begins to potter, urge him on; animate him to rush as swiftly as possible into a stanch point on the body scent of the birds.

The moment a dog puts his nose to the ground and displays a

disposition to potter on foot scent, he should be ordered on by voice, whistle, or other means. Do not be satisfied with anything less than prompt location by body scent. It may require considerable work and abundant experience on game, but in the end all such effort will be well repaid by a dog that finds bevies or coveys quickly and positively, and does snappy work on scattered birds.

In the very beginning of this book it was emphasized that the trainer must have clearly in mind what he wants the dog to do.

Courtesy American Field, Chicago

Classy Performance by a trio of Pointer Champions. *Left to Right:* Rapid Transit, Sulu, and Timbuctoo

In reference to the proper handling of game, let us include the following remarks made by the late Dr. Percy R. Bolton, for many years president of the Continental Field Trial Club and a recognized authority on bird dog values.

"An accurate description as to what constitutes class in bird work should consist, not of anyone's ideals, but of the way in which the 100 per cent dog finds and handles game, followed by mention of the moves he does not make in the process.

"There are obviously few dogs, even successful winners, that fill the bill entirely, but they do exist and their methods should form the standard for this most important function of the bird dog.

"To be accurate, however, any description of what the dog does in the presence of game necessitates taking into account the circumstances under which he finds it, for his method varies with conditions up to the moment when he establishes his definitive point.

"Let us suppose that the dog's ground work has led him to cover holding birds and he scents them. His manner changes at once by an increase in animation and in caution and then, depending upon the direction of the wind or the entire absence of wind, he adopts different ways of locating and pointing his quarry.

1. If he is to leeward of it, i.e., if the wind is blowing from it toward him, he turns, moves directly into the wind and approaches the game to the proper distance and points directly at his birds.

In this variety of locating and pointing there is little or no reduction in speed and no lowering of the head.

2. If he is not to leeward of the game the dog pursues a different strategy. He reduces his speed somewhat and with prudence moves this way and that in search of a lead. If no clew is discovered promptly he at once and with speed proceeds to circle the position at which he first got scent. In this way he either gets to leeward of the birds and then moves up wind to point as before, or he crosses the trail of the birds, if they are moving, and then circles again, repeating the process until he is able to go up wind to his point.

In this method of locating and pointing there is a little reduction in speed on the short casts, but none on the circling and no lowering of the head.

3. If there is no wind at all the dog reduces his speed somewhat and with caution makes short casts in various directions, and occasionally lowers his head to estimate the increasing or diminishing scent on the ground or vegetation until he assures himself of the probable position of his game, when he moves directly to it or makes his final locating by circling. Under these conditions there may be a material reduction in speed and an occasional lowering of the head without demerit.

4. If birds are in the open feeding, or scattered, or in unlikely places and their scent suddenly recognized by the dog running at full speed, he stops instantly, locates and points without any preliminary moves at all.

"Under the first three conditions the maneuvers of the dog are logical, studied and easily comprehended by the onlooker; and once the game is located accurately in distance and direction the dog flashes into a rigid, intense and attractive attitude, upstanding, with head and tail high.

"Under the fourth condition, as has been said, the reflex of the scent galvanizes the dog in almost any position, but the intensity is there and so is the accuracy of location.

"This constitutes class in bird work and should coexist with class in ground work, that is, bird sense, speed, range and endurance in the finished dog; and the way in which he handles game when he does it correctly forms one of, and probably the most, agreeable spectacles of field performance.

"The reverse is true as well, for who cares to watch the pottering grass-prowler back and fill in foot-scent or see birds incorrectly located or blinked or flushed, or what is there appealing in the dog which is limp on his points or points with low head and tail, or which lies or sits down or points with wagging flag, or habitually false points or commits others of the long list of errors in handling game?

"Certainly bringing game to the gun is the ultimate function of the bird dog and his reason for being, so that correct and pleasing work in finding and pointing class, should receive its full credit and indeed higher credit than it does at present in the comparative rating of field trial competitors."

CHAPTER XXI

Backing

"Backing," in sporting parlance, means honoring the stand of a bracemate. It is, in fact, pointing without actual scent of game but in acknowledgment of the point of another dog which is in sight. Thus a dog is said to back when he halts without having seen or scented game, but does so because he sees another dog on point nearby. A majority of bird dogs do this instinctively, a natural reaction when coming upon another dog on point, although there are some dogs of jealous disposition which abhor the act of backing and will not do so voluntarily, and are even reluctant to do so at command.

After your dog is schooled perfectly in steadiness to wing and shot, it is time to start working him with a reliable bracemate. More than likely, the pupil will perform the act of backing spontaneously. Many dogs back at sight the first time they see a bracemate on point. The development of the gift rests with the trainer. This may be accomplished by a procedure similar to that used when making the dog stanch on point.

Work the pupil with an experienced dog, one sure of nose, positive in his location of game, and upstanding on point. When you are ready to give the lesson in backing, do not rely on an unsteady dog as a bracemate for your pupil. The results might be disconcerting. Use only a well broken, rock steady companion.

When the old dog establishes a point, the pupil is brought into the vicinity in such a manner that he will catch sight of his bracemate on point before he can actually scent the birds. If he evinces an inclination to hesitate cr back, the educator can steady him just as when he was teaching stanchness on point. Do not feel nervous or think that your pupil will fail to back. Don't confuse him with incessant coaching. Until you have determined definitely that he is of the green-eyed variety that does not take naturally to backing, have full confidence that he will do so as a natural action under normal circumstances.

Backing the point of a bracemate, from the standpoint of usefulness to the gunner, serves the purpose of preventing another dog from coming into the vicinity and flushing the quarry a bracemate

Courtesy American Field, Chicago

Honoring a Bracemate's Point

is pointing. This action under certain conditions makes for ordered operations in the hunting field. There is no more picturesque and beautiful sight than that of a bird dog pointing loftily with several other dogs honoring stylishly, each backing proudly, confidently. Spanish sportsmen call the act patronizing, which is a rather descriptive term.

Should your pupil fail to back with utmost naturalness, but rather advances until he himself gets the scent of the birds, or perhaps even passes the pointing dog and disturbs the game, consider it something in the ordinary course of events. But on the next find by the experienced bracemate, bring the young dog into the vicinity again. Just at the instant that the pupil catches sight of the old dog on point, utter the youngster's name smartly. The effect is likely to be exactly what you want. The combination of seeing the bracemate on point and having his own name spoken sharply undoubtedly will cause the pupil to stiffen into a back. Do not miss the right moment. If you start to coach and caution before the pupil has caught sight of the dog on point, some of the effect will be lost. Be careful, too, not to delay your part too long. This is another case where "timing" is all-important, like in driving a golf ball 250 yards down the fairway.

In the event that your dog does not back properly when this procedure has been followed, fasten the check cord to his collar and on the next occasion lead him up behind the pointing dog. Do this without letting the young dog scent the game. If he is brought up from directly in the rear, bring him to a back several rods away. If you have a helper, have him keep the dog in position; otherwise tie the cord to something available to restrain the pupil, then advance and flush the birds. Rarely, indeed, does one encounter a dog that fails to acquire the idea of backing very readily after he has once honored a bracemate's point and seen the birds flushed from in front of his companion.

In case a dog is of jealous disposition and will not honor another dog's point voluntarily, it is generally necessary for the trainer to resort to the check cord and compel the pupil to back his bracemate's point. This is really "stopping at command." It is never a spontaneous gesture or true back with such dogs, but merely a result of obedience training. We have seen quite a few dogs which, as the result of well developed intellect, back at sight when the handler is in the vicinity, but when out of view will invariably "steal the point" of the other dog!

When schooling the young dog to back, there should be no doubt of the point of the bracemate. Do not ask the pupil to back what is surmised to be a false point. No dog likes to do this. Many resent it, although some may do it as the result of disciplinary measures. In the case of field trial competition, the question of backing a false point has been a source of much discussion among professional handlers and judges. Some insist that the dog should do it as an exemplification of training, whereas others contend that if the dog snaps into a back at sight, then proceeds warily until he has the advantage of the wind, whereupon if he does not scent game, no error is to be charged if he goes on about his hunting and the bracemate's point is proved unproductive.

CHAPTER XXII

Undesirable Tendencies and Faults

Intelligent direction of the hunting dog's education will keep the pupil from acquiring bad manners or serious faults. Certainly it is up to the trainer to anticipate, if at all possible, the development of undesirable traits on the part of the dog and to forestall such an eventuality. The system of training outlined in preceding chapters is designed to prevent formation of harmful habits on the part of the canine pupil and it might be worthwhile to reiterate that the amateur trainer who early discovers serious shortcomings in his prospect would be much better off to give him away and get an unspoiled one rather than to attempt to overcome major faults. While corrective measures can be applied successfully, in 99 cases out of 100 the process is long drawn out and the results scarcely worth the time and tedious effort.

POTTERING

Something has been said previously about overcoming any drift on the part of the dog to potter. This is largely a matter of training. The alert, energetic, hard-working handler is not likely to develop a pottering dog, but an indifferent instructor of torpid temperament may transform an ambitious, fast, snappy dog into a confirmed potterer. Prevention of the fault is relatively simple; the handler must incite the dog to hunt at a lively clip, be quick to urge him on if there is the least inclination to linger or prowl, guard against the pupil fussing unduly with sparrows and field larks, and avoid the temptation to "Whoa" the dog into point on foot scent. See Chapter XX.

If the dog does show pottering tendencies, energetic measures on the part of the educator are called for; he must be alert to see that the dog moves at a good rate of speed, that the canine searches with nose in the air for body scent. The trainer must proceed at a pace swift enough to keep the dog on the jump out in front, and if the dog begins to tarry or sniff about, he must immediately be urged to go on. True, such driving tactics carried to excess can be responsible for the development of a dog that merely runs, rather than hunts, but it is up to the trainer to control this. Working the

A pair of Pointer field trial winners

dog from horseback many times will have a salutary effect; it inspires the dog to hunt with greater celerity.

TRAILING

Initiative is a wonderful talent. It is the energy or aptitude for bold action that tends to develop a worthwhile objective; in a phrase, it is self-reliant enterprise. The person possessed of marked initiative is thrice blessed. No less so with the hunting dog. It sets off the noteworthy performer.

A dog lacking intrepidity and independence, if worked with a bracemate, may early disclose trailing propensities. Many trainers work young dogs with old campaigners to cultivate bird sense in the prospects. This may work out most advantageously with extremely independent prospects, or again it may militate against a youngster's proper development. Numerous puppies are intensely imitative when they associate with older dogs. If you hunt a puppy with an older dog, you may notice that the youngster is inclined to follow his experienced companion. If the old dog casts one way, the pup follows him. If the old dog points, the prospect may point along-

A scene to delight the heart of any hunter and bring a sense of pride to the trainer of these Pointers

side or even back him, and very likely the novice trainer thinks that such a juvenile is the finest kind of material for development into a first-class hunting dog. But the veteran knows otherwise. Just as soon as he notices a puppy acting in this manner, he will cease working him in the company of an older dog, for he realizes that there is grave danger that the youngster will soon come to rely on his experienced bracemate to locate the game. A skilled trainer will hunt the juvenile alone thereafter in the effort to inspire that independence of spirit which will prompt the dog to seek the birds himself.

Again, a dog with a lesser flight of speed than his canine companion may consistently run behind the bracemate.

One should not confuse the competitive inclination to race a bracemate with trailing. Especially in field trials, one may come across a dog that runs alongside or even in the wake of his bracemate for a long distance; this is not trailing in the true sense, but merely a manifestation of the competitive spirit, an urge to test his speed against his hunting adversary.

Any prospect which displays true trailing tendencies—whether he tails his bracemate, is a head-on trailer, or in any wise uses the initiative of his bracemate to find game—should at all times be hunted alone. Take him out by himself, let his hunting instincts ripen, firmly establish his confidence in his own abilities to locate game, and stimulate his interest by killing birds over his points. Until his independence is completely confirmed, and he shows ambition to seek out birdy places on his own, do not work him with other dogs.

FALSE POINTING

The dog which continually false points is a source of no small annoyance to the gunner. Faulty training fosters this serious shortcoming. Permitting a graduate dog to stop on ground sparrows, meadow larks, etc., promotes this delinquency. The dog which will point stanchly on such unwarranted stimulus, or without any real rime or reason, nevertheless can be made into a useful hunting companion if he has a proper degree of intelligence.

The reasons for the growth of this habit may be different, but in the majority of cases false pointing can be ascribed to the fact that the owner or trainer was so pleased when the dog displayed an inclination to point with or without game, that the dog was permitted, even encouraged, to do this frequently, the pupil soon believing the point was what his master wished regardless of the presence or absence of game. Over-training is chiefly responsible. The dog is made overly cautious around game and feels obligated to point the slightest scent he may encounter.

We recall an experience with a handsome and very typey pointer dog. It was a dandy Fall day and we were out where an opportunity for pheasants—maybe some Hungarian partridges—would be afforded. It is an invariable practice not to have more than two guns in the party bird shooting. The owner of the pointer started out with us, his hopes high, and he boasted with understandable pride about a splendid job the dog had done just a couple of days before. It was going to be a beautiful day, according to the promise of the morning, and the dog, Tuck, would surely provide some excellent sport. Tuck loped off in a pipe-opener, then cut back toward us and started to work the country ahead. We were on foot, so the dog adjusted his range properly. Suddenly, about 200 yards ahead, Tuck styled up on a beautiful point. He was a picture. We admired the way he snapped into this stand; no dilly-dallying, no feathering, just a sudden stop in a pretty pose—"Here they are, boss!"

The owner glanced over at us. "He's got 'em," he declared with confidence, "let's go!" We quickened our pace, but with a finished All-Age dog there is no need for undue haste—at least, there should not be—so I did not quite match the stride of the owner. Just as Tom approached, the dog broke his point and dashed forward about forty or fifty yards, where he established another point. The owner plunged on, and the same thing was repeated. The dog would stand rigidly, every muscle tense, his attention evidently fixed on the game scent ahead; but when his owner got within a few paces of him, he would dart along some fifty yards and point again. "Must be a pheasant and it's running from him," Tom volunteered, and when Tuck snapped into another point a little distance ahead, Tom broke into a run. We let him go. To cut this short, the pointer led Tom a merry chase over much of a sixty-acre field, and was Tom's tongue hanging out when the dog decided he had enough of pointing and just went off romping out in front! Tuck, to put it brutally, was a confirmed false pointer. Evidently his owner could not tell by the dog's attitude, his emotional expression, when Tuck actually had game—or was merely pointing on suspicion. We never hunted with Tuck again, so did not seek to discover some little thing about his false points which would make the situation known to us.

But what made the dog a false pointer? Faulty early training? Innate overcautiousness? In a sense, the former, although in this particular instance, Tuck enjoyed the attention he gained and the excitement evoked by his points. The owner seemed never to catch on. He always dashed up with the greatest confidence that Tuck had 'em pinned, and no matter how often and how badly the dog fooled him, he'd go pell mell to the next "point." Tuck liked the way this was played; he pretended to point game and his owner would come dashing up, Tuck's cue to move ahead a short distance, when the owner would pant forward, and the maneuver be repeated. Tuck always kept this up until the routine got a trifle dull, and then he'd romp off for a spell, but when the mood struck him again, he would once more start false pointing all over the place.

In such a case, an almost sure cure is to ignore the dog's points. Don't pay the slightest attention to him. The "vanity" point is a

A stylish point is backed with beautiful manners by two other dogs to complete a picture the sportsman will long remember

simple case and routine treatment is to shame the dog out of such false points. Pay no attention until you know he actually is pointing game. When he points, merely go on quietly without notice; the dog must understand that the mere act of pointing will not win commendation; that he must establish a stand only on game birds. Maybe, before you can tell positively from his emotional expression, the dog will actually have birds and you will have simply gone on. What of it? The chances are that when this does happen, the dog will hold this point stanchly.

False pointing due to over-cautiousness is mostly chargeable to inept early training. To overcome this ordinarily means a "re-breaking" process. You have got to get the dog keen again, make him bold, erase all signs of extreme cautiousness, even encourage him to chase his birds. You seek to get him to dash boldly into point on game and when this has been accomplished then follow the original procedure of steadying him, this time being sure to avoid any chance of instilling timidity.

Many times an otherwise promising dog will have the failing of wanting to point everything he comes across. Any vagrant scent may stop him. If the cause is other than a faulty nose, the remedy can be found, though it may mean studying your canine pupil with greatest care. There was the instance of a well known and successful professional bird dog trainer, prominent in major trials, who was confronted with the problem of a false-pointing dog which, if that shortcoming could be overcome, would have been a dangerous contender in the leading championships. Indiscreet early training had caused it. A good sharp command, "Whoa," was sufficient to make this dog snap into a point. Opposing handlers knew all about it and in a one-course trial when the bird field was reached, the handler of the other dog would shout "Whoa," a few times at his own dog, but Ben would stop and point. After this happened repeatedly, Ben was out of the stake, naturally.

How could Ben's failing be corrected? For a full season the handler studied over what might be done. Finally he hit on a plan; at least, something worth trying, he thought. He had the pointer on the Canadian prairies at the time and for the dog's next workout, the handler placed a big chew of tobacco in his mouth. He crowded the cut into his cheek and proceeded to work it into a dampened mass from which tobacco juice flowed freely. Suddenly out in front Ben pointed and the handler knew it was a false alarm. He had tried the "shaming stunt" without success, incidentally. Now he had a different idea. First of all, he went out ahead of the dog, walked well in front and around in a pretended attempt to flush, then returned to Ben, which was still pointing. Taking the tobacco from his mouth, he opened Ben's jaws and thrust the wad down into his throat. Ben gulped—*once!* "You should have seen that dog," related the trainer. "He just didn't know what had happened to him. He jumped, rolled and bounced around, and it was several minutes before he calmed down.

"After a short time we started off hunting again and it was not long until Ben actually found and pointed a covey of prairie chicken. I knew he had birds and was careful when flushing to kill one for him. I let Ben have it; he mouthed it and then I gave him his favorite parts. The dog didn't make another false point that afternoon. But a couple of days later, Ben did establish a stand where I could tell he didn't have birds. But I had a chew all ready for him. The performance was repeated and Ben didn't like that second dose any better than he had the first one. On his next actual covey find, I killed a bird for him—and again let him have it. I was trying to make him understand that when he pointed and really had game,

Lindsay Photo Service

Nine Woodcock and eight Ruffed Grouse taken over the points of this Pointer and Setter

he would be rewarded; that was what I wanted him to do. But if he came to a stand without birds in front of his point, something unpleasant was going to happen to him. I think that he got the idea after absorbing that second chew. At any rate, he did not make a single false point on the prairies the rest of that season, won one of the biggest All-Age stakes in Canada, and except for the fact that his owner retired him for stud purposes, I believe the dog would have won some important quail events, too."

The kernel of the whole experience is, "I tried to make him *understand.*" It is up to the trainer to find out as much as possible about his canine pupil's psychological processes, to determine just what may prompt the dog to do certain things that are wrong, and he must then endeavor to devise some means to make the dog comprehend exactly what is expected of him.

Speaking of false points, the novice trainer is cautioned not to condemn his dog in too great haste. Don't jump to the conclusion that your dog is a confirmed false-pointer just because you fail to produce game in front of some of his points. A number of unusual things can happen. We have a disposition to recite several extraordinary occurrences, but the following should suffice to convince the novice handler that there are occasions when the dog can be given the benefit of the doubt. It happened during a three-hour heat in the National Club's Free-for-All Championship in 1922, involving Doughboy, a celebrated field trial champion.

Doughboy made a cast around a clump of bushes and was seen to point. A few spectators riding to one side had a good opportunity to see the dog just as he froze into his point, but from the position the judges were in it is doubtful if they did. Martin, Doughboy's handler, called point and started riding to him, but he also probably did not see what happened just then. The dog had been standing only a few moments when a hawk swooped down just in front of him and up went a bevy of birds. It could not be determined whether the hawk was successful in securing a quail, but in any event, seeing the crowd gallop up, the hawk soared away, while Doughboy remained rigidly on point. Martin walked all about the dog, endeavoring to flush, so it was evident that he did not see what happened and failing to produce birds, as was natural, he sent Doughboy on, and it is probable that the dog was charged with an unproductive point. It was only some time later that Martin learned just what happened, although he did see the hawk as it soared away and probably drew his own inferences. It is just possible that the judges also saw the predatory bird in that vicinity, though, of course, no one knew just what conclusions they drew from that.

This is only one of the many incidents that occur in field trials or may happen in the shooting field, so where one does not always obtain an exact definition of the work, be charitable.

CHAPTER XXIII

Blinking, Bolting, Rabbit Chasing

"Blinking" is the most serious sin in the bird dog Decalogue, No. 1
of the "Thou shalt nots." It is a result of incorrect, and oftentimes
brutal, training methods.

There are different degrees of blinking. There is the dog which
searches industriously enough and when he locates birds, will point
stanchly. But as the handler approaches, the dog will semi-circle to
the opposite side and establish another point. Indeed, the dog may
shift his position several times, knowing exactly where the birds are
all the time and such shifting is not an effort on the part of the dog
to gain a more advantageous position from standpoint of wind direction to strengthen scent perception and improve accuracy of location. The novice should be careful in the analysis of such work.
If it is a pure case of fidgeting, or what may be described as a preliminary act in the development of blinking, careful handling is
necessary to overcome this. The dog must be forced to stay stanchly
where he pointed originally; just as soon as any inclination to move
is exhibited, "Whoa" is commanded and the dog compelled to stand
his ground. If the dog is of the type that does not alter his point
position until you come up close behind him, make it a practice
to circle at a distance so that you will approach him from in front
as you prepare to flush. We have known field trial performers and
worked gun dogs which always wanted to be facing the person who
approached to flush the birds. This is not blinking in a precise sense.
In one specific instance of quite a celebrated setter, the dog deduced
that if the handler came walking toward him to flush the game, the
birds would invariably fly back over his point and he would have
an opportunity to whirl and chase. He knew from experience that

185

if when breaking he had to charge past his handler, punishment would be meted out immediately, but when the birds came back over his pointing position with the handler out ahead, he could wheel and have a fling at pursuit without liability to pay an immediate penalty.

A certain stage of blinking is when the dog leaves his point as the trainer nears, slinks back to the handler and with unmistakable timidity follows at heel as the trainer walks to where the dog had pointed the birds. Fear of making a mistake sometimes prompts this action; the dog does not know exactly what he should do. The wrong kind of early education confused him. Perhaps on one of his first points the gunner had rushed up, commanded loudly and frequently, "Whoa, Steady," made a pass or two at the dog with a switch, flushed the birds, fired a volley, forced the dog to drop and in general so frightened the poor creature that he certainly doesn't want any part of a similar performance again. The form of blinking where the dog breaks his point to come back to his handler is curable, although the remedy to correct this necessarily takes considerable time, patience, experience. Encouragement is called for, not restraint. Work the pupil with older dogs which show great enthusiasm, even those which break shot, and it is also well to teach the timid prospect to retrieve.

There are dogs which blink birds in still another manner. One of this type will range freely, hunt energetically, then when coming upon game will feather and point, then shortly leave the location and go on ranging in search of other birds. Such dogs may do this right after being put down, but later hold their points with utmost stanchness. One dog we recall always blinked the first bevy of the day in just that manner, but performed faultlessly thereafter.

Another blinking type is the dog which coming upon birds, merely drops his tail, glances furtively about and gives a general appearance of unhappiness because of having encountered the scent of game, then cautiously swings to the side and promptly goes on.

But the worst form of blinking—sometimes quite difficult to detect and almost impossible to correct—is that of the dog which when searching becomes conscious of the effluvia of game, but passes by with scarcely a perceptible sign, merely ducking to one side or the other as he skirts the cover to avoid flushing the birds.

Dogs in various stages of this fault have been cured and made into useful performers. It is a tedious process and unless enough time and attention can be devoted to the single dog, success is not likely to result. For this reason, most veteran handlers deem it better to forego any attempt to train a dog which has become a blinker, and authorities recommend that the amateur who wants to try his hand at dog training get an unspoiled prospect and work him. However, for the benefit of some readers who may have such great faith in a particular dog that they want to attempt correction of a tendency to blink, the case of Jay R's Boy, famous setter champion, might be cited.

In his Derby form—while still under two years of age—Jay R's Boy won premier laurels in the Tenth American Field Quail Futurity, following which he dropped from the limelight owing to serious faults. It was noised about the field trial circuit that the setter had become a blinker! Ed Farrior, when he launched his career as a professional handler, persuaded Dr. T. H. Clark of Golconda, Illinois, the owner of Boy, to send the setter to him. Farrior had seen the dog during his Derby season and was familiar with the faults that had cropped up, but felt he could correct the shortcomings and make the dog a real contender. The success of Farrior's efforts may be adjudged when it is said that Jay R's Boy was piloted to a double championship, winning the National Free-for-All title in 1919 and acccounting for that crown again in 1920.

"It wasn't easy to make a bird dog of Jay R's Boy," Ed Farrior told us, "but the trick was done by killing a sack of birds about every day over some of my other dogs, with Boy backing them from the end of a rope held by a helper. A darky led the dog hundreds of miles, but the end was worthy of the means, for when I made good with Boy, my future as a professional was assured.

"We gunned over a lot of my other dogs and I had my colored helper bring Boy up whenever game was pointed. Boy didn't take any interest at all to begin with, but the evident enthusiasm of the other dogs in locating quail and the satisfaction they displayed when birds were killed over their points soon got the setter keen to have a part in it. Of course, the helper never spoke to the dog at all; just led him up, made no attempt to reassure him, never any fuss to get Boy keyed up. That came gradually. Thereafter, with careful work and killing birds for Boy, he became mighty eager to find game."

Ed Farrior indisputably ranks with the most successful field trial handlers of pointers and setters of all time, and he still gets a thrill out of developing a good one down at L. D. Johnson's Wildfair Plantations, Albany, Ga. "You can't help but feel pretty good when you bring out a new winner," declared Ed, "and there is a great deal of satisfaction in the knowledge that you have taken the raw material, molded and developed it along your own lines and finished the job properly. It is mighty fascinating to watch a dog improving all the time, to witness the development of his natural qualities. It takes considerable time, patience and skill to get a fiery, impetuous youngster right to win in Derbies, leaving him bold and snappy on his game.

"My idea of a high-class bird dog," he continued, "is one that hunts intelligently, is bold and goes to his game with snap and dash. I consider a good field trial dog is a good shooting dog, and train mine accordingly. I use judgment as to who shall shoot over my dogs, but when a friend comes along wanting to kill a few quail, I always take my field trial dogs out to provide the shooting and they always deliver satisfactorily. Incidentally, I think prairie training is the very best there is, the most desirable of all forms of work, and that one month spent on the Canadian prairies is worth more than twice the time in any other place, especially for a Derby prospect."

BOLTING

"Bolting" is a manifestation of the desire to self-hunt. The bolter is utterly unreliable as a gun dog. There are different schools of thought on what causes a hunting dog to grow into a bolter, some ascribing it to too much liberty in early life, the dog becoming an outlaw confirmed in self-hunting so that he is impatient of any restraint whatsoever, habitually going out of his handler's control and not returning until he has satisfied his self-hunting urge. Others contend that not such freedom but our present system of field trials produced the bolter. Be that as it may, unquestionably the driving tactics of a certain type of handler has helped promote the appearance of such dogs in field trials. Whatever the cause, the trainer of bird dogs is occasionally confronted with a pupil which, if not a confirmed bolter, has strong leanings in that direction.

As a general but not invariable rule, a bolter is a headstrong, unusually bold and fearless dog, possessed of extraordinary hunting enthusiasm, great pace and marked stamina. If such a strong willed, valiant dog can be properly disciplined, the trainer is likely to have a formidable contender in any kind of competition, though as a matter of experience it must be stated that it is only with the greatest difficulty that bolting tendencies can be eradicated and occasionally there are dogs which resist the most ingenious methods of overcoming such inclinations.

There are some dogs of such extraordinary independence of spirit and high fortitude that on their own initiative they will range out of sight and continue hunting on their own, completely working a wide area before returning to locate their handler, perhaps picking him up by following his trail. Such dogs are not confirmed bolters in the true sense. With a lot of work and careful attention on the part of a seasoned professional they will indubitably become expert hunting dogs.

Bolters ordinarily act in one of two ways. First, the dog will start slowly, swing to his handler very obediently at the outset, working in the direction the trainer indicates, but just as soon as opportunity permits, such as topping a rise or getting on the far side of a copse, the dog will head for parts unknown and remain out of control, paying not the slightest heed to any whistling or shouting on the part of the handler. Some dogs get pretty "cute" in this way. Ray Smith, the professional of Somerville, Tennessee, had a very stylish setter that caused Ray to lie awake at night and to ride like a demon during the day to defeat the dog's bolting tendencies.

The usual treatment for this type of bolter is a job for the strict disciplinarian. The dog must be drilled in the obedience lessons, schooled thoroughly in every phase of yard training. Strong measures may be indicated, but since the dog is filled with an overwhelming urge to hunt, his boldness ordinarily will permit the trainer to apply such severe tactics without quenching the ambition to search for game.

One more example of bolting is that exhibited by the dog which races away as fast as his legs will carry him, is utterly heedless of his handler, but goes on a self-hunting spree that may last the whole day or even longer. To bring such a bolter under control is quite an assignment, but it can and has been done. We recall an amazingly independent and headstrong pointer bitch that had become an habitual bolter and successfully resisted the best efforts of several different professional trainers to eradicate this lawlessness. She was finally turned over to Tom Lunsford of Ewing, Illinois. He applied the approved technique of having his assistants gallop her down each time she sought to get away on her own. Lunsford and two helpers made careful preparations. One of the latter was stationed well out to the left, the second helper placed a considerable distance to the right, while the chief handler released the pointer bitch, Belle, in the middle of the course. When Belle cast to the boundary of the course on the right, the assistant who was lying in wait in that direction quickly rode her down and whipped her back to Lunsford's control. A similar procedure was followed when she got to the limits of the course on the left. The idea was to make the bitch understand that she could hunt freely only when out in front of her regular boss and that she was expected to respond to his directions. It was a tough task for Tom Lunsford and his chief assistant, "Doc" Elton McDuffy; several good horses were used up and much skillful horsemanship required, but they got the job done right.

The late James M. Avent, the "Fox of Hickory Valley," Tennessee, one of the most successful handlers in the history of the field trial sport, employed a hound, "Ringwood," to trail any of his dogs which were disposed to bolt. When a dog went out of sight and did not return within a reasonable time, "Uncle Jim" laid the hound to the trail and Ringwood, like the Royal Canadian Mounted, never failed to get his *man!* The late Charlie Babcock used a hound in similar manner and the celebrated handler and author, Er Shelley, did likewise.

Another effective method is to put a check cord on a dog with bolting tendencies and have him led around behind some reliable gun dogs, permitting him to back their points and watch the shooting. This technique is similar to that adopted for curing gun-shyness and blinking.

HANDLING POINTING DOGS ON FUR

The experienced trainer oftentimes follows the same procedure with rabbits that he does in the case of chickens. That is to say, handlers try to have juvenile prospects placed where barnyard fowl are plentiful so that the puppies while they grow up become accustomed to the chickens and can be readily taught to leave them alone. If it is practical, the instructor may place his prospect in a pen where there are rabbits, taking care to allow small openings as avenues of escape for the bunnies. If the dog chases the hares, he is to be punished until he understands that it isn't according to Hoyle for him to pursue Br'er rabbit.

Another method practiced by some, one that gets good results quite quickly and without endangering the hunting inclinations of the dog, is to never pay any attention to rabbits in the field. If the dog happens to point a rabbit, never shoot at the cottontail. Simply admonish the canine quietly, lead him away from the place and resume hunting for birds. Let the dog come to know that you are not at all interested in bunnies. When your pupil displays any tendency to fuss on rabbit scent, command "Leave it," and compel the dog to go off in search of birds. It is fun for the dog to chase any rabbit he starts, but after he has been given thorough yard training, it is not especially difficult to order, "Whoa," and curb this desire.

Some experts recommend that the first rabbit the dog starts should be shot by the handler. Quietly, without a command of any kind, the handler should pick up the bunny and beat the dog about the face and head with the corpse. The next time the dog causes a rabbit to hop off in alarm, a similar scene is enacted. Ordinarily a few doses of such medicine will prove effective. An adaptation of this plan, if the trainer wishes, is to tie the rabbit remains to the dog's collar until he becomes so thoroughly disgusted that the dog will want nothing whatever to do with furred fauna.

Jack rabbits on the Canadian prairies are an irresistible temptation to most dogs, but there, with an abundance of jacks and the fact that these nimble creatures can commonly outspeed the dog, plus the ability of a well mounted handler to ride the canine down and whip him off, the matter of breaking the jack chasing impulse does not cause the professional undue concern.

CHAPTER XXIV

Full Development of Latent Qualities

There are ways and means of developing the bird dog's potentialities, methods which will bring to fruition the latent qualities of the dog and assure performance of the highest class in every respect. Some dogs which range moderately in open country can be induced to broaden the scope of their casts until they cover as much territory as a fast stepping and wide going field trial dog. Different systems of accomplishing this can be used, depending on the individual dog. Actually, sending a setter or pointer to Canada for Summer training on sharp-tailed grouse in the prairie provinces is the best way to bring out the full talents of the prospect. There in the "chicken" country conditions are right to encourage the dog to step out in search of game, the handler can keep his canine charge under almost constant observation, permitting the instructor to anticipate and correct incipient faults and advance the dog's education along the most beneficial lines. When young, the sharp-tailed grouse, commonly referred to as prairie chicken, is an ideal bird for working prospects. The immature chickens fly only a short distance and thus repeated opportunities to locate can be easily afforded the dog. Besides, wise old prairie cock birds will teach the canine scholar much that shall prove valuable to him in solving scent situations and matching wits against a feathered quarry. This experience will apply not only when he is searching for sharp-tailed grouse, but also when hunting for quail, ringneck pheasants, and even ruffed grouse.

If the reader considers his dog a field trial prospect, we cannot recommend too strongly that he give the youngster the benefit of at least one season on the prairies, preferably in the hands of an established professional handler. The results usually prove most beneficial. Such experience will stand the dog in good stead later on, whether he competes in field trials or is used exclusively for shooting purposes. Because the majority of field trial handlers adhere to the training system described in this book, when your dog is returned to you from the professional to whom this important phase of the dog's education has been entrusted, you can go right on with the instruction of your canine hunting companion.

The hunting technique adopted by a gun dog must be adjusted to

Prairie training. Note check cord on Pointer which is being given the benefit of work on sharp-tailed grouse in Canada's prairie provinces

the kind of game bird he is seeking and the character of cover being negotiated. In the ultimate analysis, the function of the bird dog is to find game for the gun. Any performance standard must be predi-cated on this, and the dog trained accordingly.

When searching for ruffed grouse in brush country, the ideal performer is a dog that reports to his handler regularly, searches both sides of the trail in approved form and generally adjusts his range to the demands of the quest. While absolutely mechanical quartering is not called for on the part of the ruffed grouse specialist, it is essential that he negotiates brushy areas quite closely for all of such regions may be productive. When hunting for quail, on the other hand, the dog may—indeed, he should—rapidly pass over un-

Photo by W. Eugene Smith

Make a "Buddy" of your hunting dog

promising terrain and direct his search to alluring objectives, and the canine hunting in natural bob-white country which quarters in the true sense is expending a lot of energy needlessly and in fruitless quest. The prairie chicken searcher, not unlike the quail performer, can also range to the coverts most likely to harbor sharp-tailec grouse, although wide side to side sweeps are desired in the relatively short grass of typical prairie country.

The ideal pheasant dog approaches in range a happy medium between the quail and ruffed grouse dog. The performer on ringnecks is necessarily different in his methods from the grouse or quail dog. But it is not to be concluded that *per se* the high-class quail or prairie chicken dog will not prove a worker of merit on pheasants. It is in the manner of hunting the country wherein the difference lies, for where the quail dog may quickly and thoroughly wind the likely spots and thus cover a wealth of territory, the pheasant lurks in many places, even the sparse meadows, and the sagacious dog must adapt himself accordingly and hunt the fields of the course with precision. Because pheasants may be parked anywhere, it follows that there are no particularly "birdy" hideouts between which to choose. Therefore the pheasant dog should not race past unalluring fields as may the quail dog, nor is it to be desired that the pheasant dog be restricted in range and quarter regularly, much in the manner of the ruffed grouse dog. Sportsmen who shoot pheasants want a class performer; they demand style, speed, snap, and decision, intelligence and precision. The slow potterer and grass prowler that creepingly noses about on foot scent, no longer is acceptable. The fast, dashing, positive bird-finder is wanted, because such a dog has the magical faculty of wielding a hypnotic influence over these sprinters of the stubble, and a dog with intelligence and decision apparently mesmerizes them into crouching.

It might be added that while stanchness on point is desirable on the part of the quail dog, the expert pheasant dog does not exhibit a similar solidity of position if the ringneck attempts to escape by running. Effective performance on pheasants requires that the dog point only body scent, and that just as soon as the strength of the body odor begins to wane, the dog should break his point and relocate exactly.

Equally good pheasant dogs may use different tactics, but the methods of the seasoned performer on wily prairie chicken cocks are excellent for ringnecks, too. Such experts do not dally in an effort to unravel foot scent, but make short casts with nose held high, straining the wind for telltale body scent. It is a thrilling sight to watch the class dog which works in this manner. There is another type of performance, effective though not so spectacular, where the dog roads or draws in the relocation maneuver. But the wary ring-neck cock will make a monkey of the dog which puts his nose to the ground and creeps along sniffing the foot scent!

It can be said that the really high-class bird dog, given experience, automatically adjusts his technique to suit the occasion. He hunts different types of cover intelligently, wisely adapting his range. He is competent to handle each and all of the game birds he is required

Photo by W. Eugene Smith
After a good work-out in hot weather, be sure to cool off the dog with water

to hunt. There have been notable field trial performers which have won championship titles on several varieties of game—quail, prairie chickens, pheasants, and Hungarian partridges. Ruffed grouse champions have made impressive showings in competitions on other game birds. This knack of adjustment is the mark of genius in the top-flight performer.

We have emphasized earlier in this book that it is not always the dog which develops very quickly that proves the most satisfactory in maturity. The puppy prodigy, like the child phenom, many times

is only a flash-in-the-pan. In the proper unfolding of nascent indi-
cations of natural greatness, the experienced trainer does not attempt
restriction or control. Indeed, encouragement rather than restraint
may be called for to reveal to the fullest extent the superior faculties of an individual dog.

It is said that concentration and achievement are twins. Rem-
brandt and painting, Mozart and music, Burbank and plants, Ford
and automobiles, Mayo and surgery, Shakespeare and drama. All
the shining lights reached the top by concentrating on doing one
task supremely well. Nothing can stop the flaming brilliance of
undivided intense effort. This faculty is a powerful tool at the command of the intelligent dog educator. Where a trainer is able to
concentrate his efforts on the development of a single canine pupil,
extraordinary achievement is quite sure to result. The records of
public competitions prove that when an astute handler has been able
to give time and attention to a particular dog, marked success has
resulted. We cite the case of professional Chesley H. Harris, with
Carl Duffield's setter dog, Candy Kid, triple Chicken Champion;
also the same handler with the late Louis Haggin's pointer, Becky
Broom Hill, one of the trio of Triple National Champions. Ed Farrior had to put a lot of skillful effort on Jay R.'s Boy, as mentioned in
a previous chapter. Forrest Dean spent a great deal of time on
Feagin's Mohawk Pal, and succeeded in winning the National Championship three times with the E. M. Tutwiler setter. Other illus-
trations of how a handler's devotion to a particular dog paid big
dividends are common. A recent example is Amazon's Village Girl,
the pointer bitch trained and handled by Howard Kirk, which did
considerable winning for her owner, H. E. McGonigal of Kokomo,
Indiana.

Authorities on training generally agree that pointers develop more
quickly than setters. You can hurry the education of a pointer, but
it does not pay to crowd a setter if your aim is a great natural performer. While there have been instances of really brilliant dogs
which did not begin to show their true quality until in their fourth
or fifth year, we cannot support the Bill Beazell philosophy which
advocated waiting until the dog was at least four years old before
attempting to break him on his game. No good purpose is served by
letting a dog run riot past the time when the pointing instinct has
asserted itself! It nets down again to the individual dog.

While a shorthair at three or four years of age may be at the apex of his powers, it is true with most setters that they keep on getting better and not until six or seven years do the longhairs reach their zenith. In the case of Sport's Peerless Pride, winner of four titles including his spectacular victory in the 1939 National Championship, the L. M. Bobbitt setter kept on improving each season and it was not until he was over five years of age that he approached the peak of his powers. And to go back twenty years or more, Shore's Ben, setter champion, winner of the Free-for-All quail title in 1921, came on rather slowly and by laborious effort on the part of his handler. John Willard Martin was entirely responsible for Ben's development. Martin recognized that Ben was a dog that could not be pushed or hurried. He realized that the dog was endowed with marvelous potentialities, but he did not believe in crowding his pupil. Between Martin and Ben a close bond seemed to exist. The handler made the dog his boon companion and practically lived with him. On one occasion a visitor sought Martin on his training grounds; he had failed to find him at his place of abode, and so rode out over the fields. Coming to a secluded place, he fancied he heard someone talking and he slowed down and approached more cautiously. To his surprise he found Martin and Ben in a little sylvan spot, enjoying a noonday rest and a bite to eat. John was seated with the dog nearby. Ever and anon the handler passed Ben a morsel and said a few words to him; the dog seemingly understanding the "conversation." Martin was not in the least perturbed upon the appearance of his unexpected visitor nor did he or the dog shift positions, except Ben eyed the stranger somewhat curiously. "Ben and I," drawled John, "have been having a little heart-to-heart talk about the things we have to do if we want to win. Sometimes I think he's the greatest dog I ever had and then again he has me guessing. I spend a lot of time fooling with him and some days I think he has everything a high-class dog ought to have and then he pulls some new tricks that keep me awake at nights." But Martin and Ben continued their companionship and conversations in Alabama hunting environments and eventually they understood each other.

CHAPTER XXV

Significance of Field Trials

The first recorded field trial for setters and pointers took place near Stafford, England, in the Spring of 1866. That initial event was in the days before public stud books existed, but the competition gave birth to the ideal of improvement of the bird dog breeds. Field trials in this country had their inception eight years later. The inaugural public trial in the United States was held near Memphis, Tennessee, on October 8, 1874. The sport has enjoyed a steady growth, phenomenal popularity being gained during the last twenty years. There are now over 250 sportsmen's organizations which sponsor recognized bird dog trials each year. A total of 400 different programs are staged with nearly 1300 stakes being run, which bring forth 20,000 starters annually. Field trials have been fittingly described as the fastest growing recreational activity in the United States!

The standards by which performance is judged in so-called major circuit trials do not seem strictly applicable to the every-day shooting dog. The work of the latter is gauged almost entirely from the standpoint of ability to help fill the game bag. Results are scored solely on a quantitative basis; the quality of a dog's actual performance is more or less disregarded. But in field trial competition it is *quality* rather than *quantity;* the dead bird or filled game bag is no longer the yardstick. Consequently, a dog which may make half-a-dozen productive points in a trial will not be among the winners, whereas another with only two finds wins the stake. Such decisions undoubtedly confuse the field trial novitiate, but it must be remembered that the judges take many things into account. The actions of the dogs are weighed on a more intricate scale than the possibility of

199

the shots afforded. How did the dog hunt? Stylishly, enthusiastically intelligently? Did he handle the country perfectly, using the wind to advantage when approaching promising objectives? Were his finds the result of intelligent searching and did he locate his game accurately and point positively with beautiful style? All of these details are considered by the experienced judge and veteran field trial fan, but the newcomer, swayed by the frequency of the occurrence rather than the quality of the performance, has a tough time trying to figure out how it all happened.

A California bird dog trial

Not all good "shooting dogs" will make field trial winners. Yet every *real* field trial winner can prove useful as a gun dog. Do not construe this to mean that every canine which has ever started in a field trial is *per se* an A-1 shooting dog. Many no-accounts run in trials, no argument about that, and some are mere runaways which fond owners mistakenly interpret as ranging too ambitiously. But the ideal type of field trial winner is excellent for horseback hunting, and if his wire edge is dulled by regular use in shooting coverts, he will prove a remarkably fine gun dog handled afoot. The intelligent dog has instinctive adjustability. The novice who sees contenders in prairie chicken trials and the major quail competitions in the South range out to impractical distances may well doubt this, but don't be fooled! If you ever get the opportunity to have a professional field trial handler take out some of his winning dogs for you to shoot over, don't pass up the chance. You will have one of the red-letter days in your hunting experience!

The uninitiated shooter may cling to the opinion that there is something wrong with a "double standard," one for field trial performance and another for shooting dogs. Hence it is in order to consider the purpose of public trial competitions. Fundamentally, just as in the case of thoroughbred horse racing, the aim is breed

The dog wagon for a California field trial

improvement. Field trials were not instituted for the purpose of developing a class of dogs suited to the needs of the average shooter whose only interest is to fill the game bag; the original aim was to bring to public notice the performers best equipped to perpetuate the most desirable qualities possessed by the high-class field dog. Thus field trials, not unlike horse-racing, present two angles for consideration and can be regarded as (a) a spectacular form of sport; and, (b) as a basis for data on which to conduct breeding operations.

Looked at from the first viewpoint, that a field trial is a race, the spectators go there for thrills and require dogs that can produce them. Certainly a phlegmatic, unattractive grass prowler cannot stimulate the emotions. In competition a field trial dog should exhibit more than merely being a high-class shooting dog. This does not imply that bird-finding faculties should be minimized, because as we have said, the function of a bird dog is to find and point game, and one which does not is useless, whether it be a field trial or shooting dog. While at various times in the history of field trials, certain defects crept in, such as the "class craze" period when heels alone were glorified, during recent years judges have adhered to the view that no dog should be placed in All-Age trials which does not find and point birds, unless game is abnormally scarce, in which event the consensus is that no dog should be placed because of the mere fact of pointing unless he has proved particular bird-finding ability. The dog must give a showy performance in the way of sensational speed, remarkable range, and superb stamina, otherwise the spectacular part of field trials is not achieved. Remember that field trials may be classed as a race to the birds. The successful performer therefore must possess unusual pace so that he may cover a large amount of country in the short space of time allotted to him. Superior speed enables a dog to outfoot his rival bracemate, whereby he may reach promising objectives in advance of his competitor and thus enjoy opportunity to find the birds first. But mere speed may be the product of the driving system of training, a dog dashing out to great distances solely in response to his handler's orders, therefore bird dog competitions must also be considered from the second standpoint; i.e., as a basis for data on which to pursue breeding operations.

Experienced judges are not carried away by a dog that runs fast and far, but mostly in straight lines. They seek out the dog which displays desirable and transmissible bird dog characteristics in the form of natural qualities—pace, range, bird sense, nose, stamina, and style, the contender which renders a balanced performance, searches intelligently, exhibits bird-finding ability, manifests accuracy of location and intensity on point. In short, the genuine field trial dog must do more than merely get out and run in compliance with the whistle of his handler.

The fact of the matter is that in field trials the "old type bird dog" that the veterans enjoy talking about, is still the standard of excellence; the type most admired is that which looks the country over when he is led to the starting point, selects the most likely looking cover in the right place on the proper course and goes to it, the kind which keeps the wind in his face and possesses a knowledge of where birds are likely to be in the morning, at noon and in the late afternoon, with due consideration of weather conditions. The dog of aristocratic appearance with nobility of expression. Verily, the acid test of the class bird dog in field trials remains the finding and handling of game on the course subservient to his handler.

Thus we may say that the principal object of field trials is still the promotion of the high-class bird dog, that the sport aims to provide

A Triumvirate of Crack Field Trial Performers. Three A.G.C. Sage Pointers on prairie chickens. *Left to right:* Luminary, Ariel, and Morpheus. Winners of first in the American Field Quail Futurity

competition of the highest caliber among hunting dogs, to stimulate enthusiasm among owners, and to act as a practical guide for breeders by setting a high standard of excellence.

Field trials have an added significance in making the shooting public conservation minded. Pointing dog competitions especially have impressed upon devotees of field sports the fact that mere killing of game is not essential to the greatest enjoyment of thrilling outdoor sport. Field trials, which educate the sportsman to a fuller appreciation of the work of his dogs, have also proved a mighty influence in the important work of protection and propagation to assure perpetuation of our game life.

CHAPTER XXVI

Spaniel Technique and Spaniel Trials

The *modus operandi* of the hunting spaniel in the shooting field has been dealt with earlier in the book, but some repetition might be justified at this point. Spaniels are useful for all kinds of upland game and shore shooting and are especially satisfactory as retrievers. The Springer, most popular of spaniel breeds for practical hunting purposes, makes the best general utility dog, but any of the larger varieties of Cocker and the other representative spaniels are useful and very valiant dogs.

The three essentials of the spaniel are (1) to find the game; (2) not to spoil the shot, and (3) to retrieve. Upon these three things depends the success of the dog and also the work of the handler. Spaniel training requires patience and a level head on the part of the trainer. All the spaniel varieties are very intelligent animals and when properly taken in charge can be trained to perfection. The spaniel's work should be to find and start the game within gun range, and he must be equally adept on fur and feather. His style is a merry bustle and when he comes close to game his increased animation and the rapid swishing of his stub tail will indicate it, so the gunner behind him may be prepared for the shot when the game is sprung. Most trainers break their dogs to "hup" as the bird flushes or the rabbit starts from his form. At all events, as soon as the game is moved, the dog must stop instantly and remain so until he is ordered either to retrieve if the game be killed, or to move on if a miss is registered. When the order is given to fetch, he goes cheerfully to the dead game, the fall of which he has marked, and brings the bird to hand with alacrity. If the shooting should be waterfowl or shore birds, he makes a good aquatic retriever, though the Springer is best adapted for this class of work as he is better able to handle the larger varieties of ducks.

A well trained spaniel will "hup" automatically at flush of game without the least word of caution from his handler. If two or more dogs are working together they should "hup" at flush or shot and remain so until one is ordered to retrieve, and while the favored one is bringing in the quarry the others must remain quietly.

For an all around general utility dog for mixed shooting in country

Springer Spaniel and two Labrador Retrievers

where the gunner secures his game by going afoot, there are few dogs that are better than the spaniels. Springers and Cockers are also used to supplement pointer and setter work. On large plantations in the South, the pointing dogs are used to find the bevies of quail, with the spaniels, which have remained at heel of the mounted huntsmen, doing the retrieving of the dead and wounded game. This has proven an ideal arrangement.

Spaniel field trials which have increased in number and quality since the inception of this form of the sport in the United States in 1924, have proved of great educational value to American sportsmen in general, so that today the hunting procedure of representative spaniels is known to most field sports devotees. But to quote some very valuable hints for the novice given by William Arkwright in a book on Springers. Though written many years ago, the advice is pertinent to every man interested in a sporting dog. Mr. Arkwright wrote:

"And now a necessary word or two on the natural qualities, which are those qualities that the most capable master cannot put into his pupil, and without which no spaniel can become a first rater. I will enumerate them so that they will be kept in mind right through the educational course. (1) Docility, which is the wish to learn—the desire to please the master. (2) Courage, which makes a dog uncon-

Photo by W. Eugene Smith

Springer Spaniels can take obstacles in stride

scious of fatigue—which will crash through thorns and brambles and gorse—which will force him across a river at flood. (3) Nose, which really stands for keenness of scenting power combined with the sense to apply it right. (4) Style, which is chiefly merry bustle, with flashing, quivering tail—and head ever alert, now high to reach a body-scent, now low to investigate a track: attributes that are most precious to a tired man or to one vexed at a bad shot. Style exhibits itself also in work of a decisive, dashing kind; for instance, in springing a rabbit with such vehemence as to frighten it into leaving its covert post-haste. The above are the purely natural qualities, which

I believe to be hereditary, which are certainly impossible of inculcation by any breaker. There are, besides, two additional qualities that are often natural, but if not natural, that may be to a certain extent, acquired. (1) Retrieving is often inherent in a spaniel puppy, and is exhibited by a partiality for lifting anything that is handy and carrying it about. Such a puppy usually has in addition a soft, dry mouth, and he will make the best retriever of all. But many good dogs require some schooling in the retrieve, and this will vary in degree—from ordinary cajoleries to the desperate meth-

Returning at a gallop, with a pheasant

ods of the so-called French system. (2) Water-Work. Most spaniel puppies take to this naturally, but not all of them. Some do not by instinct know how to swim, others do not care for the shock of cold water. They can one and all be taught by kind firmness and perseverance, but these artificially made swimmers are never the great water dogs—with typical spaniel cork-like abilities of dealing with rock and surf and whirlpool. It is possible that a remote strain of English water spaniels is responsible for the wonderful powers of some strains, and it is well to remember that a thick, wavy, oily coat usually goes with proficiency in swimming."

The education of the spaniel in yard training follows the routine set forth in earlier chapters. Many trainers do not resort to the force system of retrieving in the case of spaniels, permitting the natural bent of the dogs to expand for this phase of their education, but the novice has assurance that if he follows religiously the retrieving steps outlined, his spaniel will be most proficient in the art of fetching game and, owing to familiarity with disciplinary measures, be prepared to do it on order at any time and under all circumstances.

Handling of the land spaniel in the shooting field has been discussed in the regular lessons which apply to the proper development of the particular dog's hunting prowess. It must be remembered that the spaniel's range is of necessity within gunshot distance, that the dog must "hup" immediately at flush or shot, and retrieve on order. The only proper position for the spaniel when delivering game to hand is to sit up directly in front of his master. The really good retriever has a tender mouth.

Spaniel trials are most interesting. They are staged in various parts of the country so that sportsfolk situated almost anywhere within the United States can, without a great deal of inconvenience or traveling a long distance, attend one of these meets and get a first-hand impression of what they are like. While spaniel trials must be conducted under more or less artificial conditions, the tests prove just how competently dogs can be trained. Field trial dogs are "exhibition" dogs, true enough, but have the basic qualities which enable elevation of breed standards and improvement of performance. Not only will the work of the canine contenders in spaniel trials prove illuminating to any one who has not previously witnessed such competition, but the important duties of official guns— the persons authorized to shoot the game—should not be overlooked.

CHAPTER XXVII

Recognized Retrievers and Non-Slip Retriever Trials

The popularity of the recognized Retriever breeds has increased many fold during the last decade. While the Chesapeake Bay Dog and the little brown American Water Spaniel for many years have been of indispensable service to the American wild-fowler, use of the Retriever breeds for land work did not gain much vogue until Retriever trials began to flourish along about the middle 1930s.

The different Retriever breeds have been discussed. This chapter is intended simply as a summation of particular points. With Labradors, Chesapeakes, Goldens, Irish Water Spaniels, et al., retrieving is instinctive. The puppies want to carry everything in their mouths as soon as they can waddle about, and they are at once ready material for conversion into useful companions for the gun. To teach Retrievers to fetch and carry is no trouble at all. Very few specialized Retriever trainers use the force system or any regular sequence of steps like those outlined in teaching a dog to fetch dead or wounded game (See Chapters XIV and XV). But for all the development of natural qualities, certain disciplinary measures are made use of so that the dog will not refuse a retrieve in the hunting field or in ducking areas.

While the simple act of fetching is done naturally, the several requirements necessary to make the non-slip Retriever useful in a sporting sense requires patience and skill on the part of the trainer. This means educating the dog to follow alertly at heel or to remain quietly on the line or in the blind without any evidence of uneasiness, to exhibit absolute steadiness to shot, be proficient in marking the fall of game, and to retrieve on order only!

In Retriever trials under the sanction of the *AMERICAN FIELD,*

Chicago, Illinois, the rules and regulations set forth that dogs are judged for

    a. Natural ability

        Nose, marking, pace, style, and drive

    b. Training

        Obedience to handler, steadiness, tender mouth, and good delivery.

Courtesy American Field, Chicago
Labrador Retriever

Nose is the greatest asset of the Retriever, without which all the other qualities are of little or no value.

Control is essential at all times and under every circumstance. A perfectly trained Retriever at work is one which never ceases to use his nose and to quarter his ground unless or until his handler signals to direct him elsewhere. Without undue noise, he should be responsive anywhere within hearing.

The Retriever which goes quickly to the fall of a bird and locates his game readily is very valuable.

It is imperative that game be delivered tenderly to hand. Hard-mouth is the most serious of Retriever faults and experienced train-ers discard dogs of confirmed hard mouth. It must be cautioned, however, that the amateur should have unmistakable proof of this fault. Circumstantial evidence can work a hardship on the dog. Just because appearances indicate a dog may have pressed down on a pheasant or duck, don't condemn him at once. David D. Elliot,

This Chesapeake Bay dog responds to the wave by his handler and dashes out to cover the "fall" and retrieve the bird

successful handler of Retrievers, writing on the subject of hard mouth, stated:

"In my opinion a dog should not be condemned for this offense unless he gives unquestionable evidence of having committed the act. What would that evidence have to be? It would have to be a bird carrying that dog's trade-mark in such a manner that there would be no doubt left: a broken back, ribs caved in and carrying the dog's tooth marks, or definite signs of his teeth work on other parts of the body.

"All of us who train Retrievers or spaniels can remember instances where almost every dog we have ever handled has at some time or another brought to us a bird carrying the marks of more than one of his fangs. The conditions under which many birds are

Chesapeake Bay dog retrieving pheasant

found gives reasonable cause of such marks even in the mouth of the most tender retrievers. . . . When a dog has to reach for his bird into heavy overlapping cover that necessitates the dog dragging his bird out, or a wounded bird that is struggling hard in the dog's mouth while being carried over rough terrain, under such circumstances it takes very slight pressure to inflict an incision on a bird.

The only evidence to accept is marks of bodily injury that could be inflicted in no accidental way but rather are conclusive evidence of hard mouth.

"The problem of hard mouth is one that requires more care, more consideration than any other part of a Retriever's work."

Other serious faults that the trainer must anticipate or correct are: (a) breaking to shot; (b) retrieving without orders. These can be avoided or overcome by the methods explained in previous chapters.

Working a Labrador in a Field trial

We all like to watch the rapid worker, the fast, classy dog which accomplishes his task with commendable celerity. But at all times the dog's sense of smell must balance his speed. Without a commensurate nose, speed is of limited value. The brainy dog will adopt a gait that corresponds with his olfactory powers under prevailing conditions of scent. Excessive speed is a decided handicap to the dog of inferior nose. The rate of speed should be that suited to getting the job done promptly and properly. These comments apply just as forcibly to pointing dogs and spaniels as to the non-slip Retrievers.

The pace of the ideal Retriever is controlled by his brains, cultured through training and experience to meet the necessity of the moment. The dog that will adjust his pace to the requirements without overmuch aid from his handler is entitled to special recognition for this superiority. The Retriever which accomplishes his work swiftly is admirable, but speed is not the primary quality.

Labrador Retriever with Ringneck pheasant

In its truest sense, ranging properly contemplates the covering of the area of the fall methodically and effectively. The ideal ranger is one which will go directly to the mark and use judgment in working out this spot. The dog which breaks away independently, refuses to respond to directions, and does his hunting out of range of the fall is undesirable.

Retrievers many times are called upon to hurdle obstacles when going to a fall or returning with the game. The majority of these will jump naturally—in fact, for most hunting dogs the command "Over" or "Get over," accompanied by a wave of the arm, will prove

sufficient. Those who have had experience with dogs escaping kennel pens, scrambling over fences thought to be sufficiently high to
preclude egress, realize that it is more of a problem to keep most
hunting dogs from topping barriers than to instruct them how to
jump. But in case instruction in jumping seems necessary, the following routine may be recommended. Any breed can be put through
the same course.

A so-called jumping board is procured. This may consist of pieces
of board an inch or two thick, eight inches high by four feet wide,
which can be set between uprights. Or if it is possible to get a regular low hurdle, such as used in collegiate track meets, this is eminently satisfactory though a trifle high for the average trainer to
step over readily.

Begin with the regular board at a convenient height for you and
the dog, say two feet. With the dog on leash, approach the hurdle
placed in a yard or open field, and without the least hesitation step
over the board while encouraging the dog to jump across. He may
be ungainly rather than graceful. Merely circle around and repeat.
Very shortly the dog will be going over the board with a sort of
bound. When he does so, order "Get Over" as a preliminary to his
jump.

The next step is to have the dog clear the board while the trainer
walks on the outside of the upright. Like the hurdles at a horse
show for jumpers, the barrier may be raised when the dog clears
the obstacle with ease and evident understanding of what is desired
of him.

You will very quickly be able to send your dog over a fence or
other obstruction with the simple command, "Get over," accompanied by the arm signal.

Once the dog has been schooled in jumping, you can encourage
him to hurdle any obstacles that may intervene when he is coming
to you in a direct line. In the case of Retrievers, this will obviate
the need of a roundabout route when delivering. Merely stand up
close behind the hurdle, call the dog to you and slap your hand
just above your knee. If you stand too far behind the obstacle,
chances are he will go around the barrier to reach you, so take up
a position where the dog will leap rather than run around the side.

Those who have attended Retriever field trials are enthusiastic
about these spectacular shows. While there must be some artificiality

in their conduct, the attempt is made to simulate natural conditions. Dogs are given land tests and water work. In All-Age stakes, the first series generally consists of double birds—two at a time—both marked retrieves, dropped within view of the dogs, but an effort is made to have "falls" well separated. The second series of examinations are ordinarily optional with the judges, consisting of uniform tests on marked or unmarked birds.

Water tests consist of shot or shackled birds, the latter preferable to enable similar conditions and distance. Birds unmarked.

No water-shyness here! This Chesapeake Bay leaps into the water after a duck

The most outstanding Retriever trial we ever witnessed took place over the estate of Thomas M. Howell near Barrington, Illinois, under the personal direction and supervision of Martin J. Hogan. This program was staged late in October, 1935, the first meet of its kind in the Middle West, and Mr. Hogan, who had judged the International Retriever Championship Trials in England for three successive years, made remarkable preparations so that conditions, prearranged though they had to be, were almost natural. While many Retriever programs have been staged since that time in different sections of the country, none has approached the excellence of that 1935 event.

Speaking of the penchant of Retrievers for carrying things, it might prove diverting to tell of an episode with dramatic human interest.

Curley was his name, an old Curly-Coated Retriever, a kindly,

Photo by W. Eugene Smith

A yellow Labrador Retriever which points! This Lab, in charge of M. J. Hogan, establishes a definite point on his game, the only dog of his breed which we know to do this

loyal canine that had been in the same family for several years. The dog belonged to a game-keeper on a large estate in England. One day the game-keeper carefully bundled up his baby daughter in the usual white shawl and started for a stroll over the broad pastures, the dog jogging along at his master's side. Coming to a hedgerow not far from the house, the man decided to examine a partridge nest he had found a day or two before in a bit of nearby cover. Accordingly he laid his human bundle down with solicitous care on the greening grass of the meadow, walked along the thorn hedge until he found a sparse spot and wormed his way through the barbs, returning on the farther side to cover where the nest was located. While engaged in examining the nest his interest was diverted by a sound that spurred him to activity. Looking up he saw a herd of twenty or more steers bearing swiftly down upon the spot where he had laid the child. A gap had been left open at the far end of the field and the cattle grazing in the pasture beyond, attracted by the white on the green grass, had come rushing over. The alarmed father leaped into action. At the cost of many scratches and some deep wounds from the wicked barbs, the man pushed and squirmed through the hedgerow to return to where the baby and dog had been, but the herd was already milling about the spot! Frantically he drove them away, but not a trace of the baby or dog was in sight. Grief and remorse engulfed him. On a dead run he made for the house, hoping that by some stroke of fate his wife had noticed the shawl-wrapped infant and carried her home. Bursting in, he made an attempt at composure while he asked his wife about the little girl. The woman had seen or heard nothing. Without pausing to answer questions the keeper dashed from the house and returned to the spot, looking vainly for some sign of the child, then he walked disconsolately toward the hedgerow, peering up and down its length. A bit of white attracted his attention and upon investigation he made a joyous discovery. There, on the far side of the hedge, was the baby, with the faithful Retriever standing guard. The infant was still sound asleep and careful scrutiny failed to reveal a single scratch. The dog had miraculously carried the baby through the thorn hedge without the slightest prick; indeed, without even disturbing her slumber! Where the shawl was fastened with a safety pin the marks of the Retriever's mouth still showed and the cloth was damp. But the little one was unharmed and it was a happy father who proudly bore the white bundle back to the house, accompanied by the wise old dog leisurely wagging his tail.

CHAPTER XXVIII

Dogs for Defense and in War Work

When we speak of dogs for defense, it is not intended to talk about the ordinary house watchdog, but rather the great service that trained dogs can render to a nation in time of war. Sporting dogs and the various working breeds have been used to great advantage in times past in various conflicts that have changed the history of the world. Even ancient monarchs frequently had their sporting packs adapted to war work, and reference to interesting sidelights of history during the early periods will reveal many wonderful feats accomplished by dogs.

Perhaps dogs came in for greater attention doing war work in World War I, 1914-1918, than ever before. The German Shepherd was trained especially by the Teutonic powers to give assistance to their armed forces. The Allied nations were no less quick to adapt canine abilities to certain services, and the Airedale Terrier as well as other breeds proved their mettle. It was notable that the pure-bred dogs came through with flying colors and scotched the thought that mongrels had greater vigor or could be better fitted to this type of work.

World War II, with the theater of conflict even more widespread than its gory predecessor, brought even more attention to dogs in military use, and this despite the fact that it was "mechanized warfare." Not only on the actual battlefields, and around munitions dumps, but in the industrial plants where production meant the winning of the battle, dogs played important roles.

The effectiveness of the dog in defense work is owing to possession of what many term a dog's "danger sense," an instinctive quality. We know of a regimental sergeant who owes his life to his sentry dog's "danger sense." The sergeant had been asleep for some time when he was roughly awakened by his dog violently pawing his face. Springing from his bed, the sergeant found the room full of gas, to the fumes of which he would have succumbed but for his dog's instinct.

The dangerous duty assigned to well coached dogs on the battle-fields required the utmost in training. How would you like to be called upon to educate your dog as some of the German trainers were required to do? A provision in secret orders from the German High Command was that if a dog failed to do its duty, the trainer himself should substitute as a courier! Under such circumstances, the dog educator wasn't likely to be slipshod in his training meth-ods; the obedience requirements and other education of the dog proved a job on which the trainer could and decidedly would con-centrate his utmost skill. Needless to say, the dogs trained under such conditions were masters in their role.

In World War II, with *blitzkrieg* the new technique, featuring mechanization of forces and the amazing mobility of *panzer* divi-sions, ruling out much outmoded strategy and routine methods, plus the use of two-way radio, many believed that dogs would be relegated to the discard. Although not used as extensively as in World War I when trench strife stabilized a front for days and even weeks at a time, dogs were used mainly for patrol and reconnais-sance, as couriers, sentries, and for locating wounded men. Dogs trained to keep contact with a task unit proved of value indicating the whereabouts of the enemy, and the acute sense of hearing and keen sense of smell enabled these dogs to be the "eyes" of a night patrol. Also dogs were taught to fare forth into "no man's land" and when wounded were located, return and lead rescuers to the spot.

A dog locating wounded on the battlefield recalls the story of two hunting dogs which were owned by a Belgian baker, and the pair went for a daily run in an adjoining woods. One night they did not return and though search was made for them, it was not until the second day that the master, searching the woods, heard a dog's loud bark. Going to the spot from whence it proceeded, he came upon the elder dog, which was alternately barking loudly and licking the foot of his companion, which had become caught in a trap. The dog had neither food nor drink for over two days, yet he remained with his wounded companion, doing his best to summon help.

When after the perfidious attack of the Nipponese at Pearl Harbor on December 7, 1941, the United States was plunged into the all-out struggle against the Axis aggressors, a nation-wide organization sprang up for the training of dogs for defense. It was recognized that the greatest service that dogs can render in war work is extending the effectiveness of guards at military establishments and industrial plants engaged in defense production, as well as to give alarm at invidious approach to important utilities, so special training clubs devoted to schooling dogs in the requirements of sentry duties came into being. It was important for the educator to keep in mind that the dog would be actually worked by someone else, hence had to be grounded in obedience work so that he would respond to proper commands given by someone other than his trainer.

Sentry dogs ordinarily are required to heel, sit, stay, come when called and give warning of the approach or presence of any stranger. They are tested in their work under all types of distraction that might be encountered if they were patroling a danger zone.

In heeling the dog must be at all times under the control of the handler, both on and off the lead. He must stay at heel on the left side of the sentry. It is not necessary for him to sit automatically when the sentry halts, but absolute steadiness rather than perfection of position is desired.

The dog in war work must demonstrate instantaneous response to both the command and signal, and his attitude should be one of complete compliance with the order. That means he should show no inclination to resent the restraint or become restive. In testing he may be required to prove himself steady for up to thirty minutes. When the dog is ordered to stay, he is expected to remain immobile, but is allowed to choose his own position.

The dogs must be taught to come when called under all circumstances and it is advisable that the training for this should include teaching the dog to come to the handler in spite of various distractions.

When at heel, the dog must give warning of the presence of any stranger by coming to attention and stopping automatically. He may bark or growl.

To obtain uniformity in the work and avoid confusion of the dogs when turned over to soldiers, set commands must prevail They are "Sit!" "Down!" "Stay!" "Heel!" and "Come!" The dog must obey all these commands at once, when spoken in a natural voice Raising the voice and repeating the commands should not be necessary when the dog is ready for service. Similarly, signals should be brief and clear, and violence in signaling is to be avoided.

A substantial portion of the training is done at night since it is at night that the services of sentry dogs are most needed. They can extend the sentinel's effectiveness by hundreds of feet because of their ability to see, hear, and smell what a man cannot. In the protection of military stores, in depots with places where saboteurs, once inside, could hide and escape the eyes of the most alert sentry, dogs have proved of exceptional value, for these enemies could not elude the keen scenting powers and hearing faculties of a properly trained "Defense Dog." During World War II, the United States Army, through the Quartermaster General, Maj. Gen. Edmund Bristol Gregory, builded an effective dog army, and "Dogs for Defense," an organization pledged to furnish trained dogs for this branch of service, distinguished itself and its members brought recognition to the effectiveness of obedience training methods.

CHAPTER XXIX

Helpful Memoranda

No puppy should be worked over the same course continually—unless for a *special reason*, such as development of range, inculcation of confidence, elimination of any fear of getting lost. A young dog worked in the same locale time after time soon covers the territory boldly, confidently, like a city motorist weaving through downtown traffic, but placed in a strange environment the dog's range and confidence may not seem up to par. Train your dog so that he will do his stuff anywhere you ask him to hunt.

————

When you train your hunting dog, have him well grounded in the first principles of the obedience lessons and he will never entirely forget his schooling. He may commit a misdemeanor now and then, but if his fundamental training is sound, all he will need ordinarily at the beginning of each season is to touch him up in certain respects. Do not forget that he must be gotten into proper condition if he is to deliver the performance of which he is capable. Road work is a wonderful conditioner.

————

If you have had your dog trained by a professional, get instructions from him about handling the particular pupil, use the same commands and signs that the professional trainer did, and follow the suggestions he may give to you.

————

A too drastic system of training will cow the majority of dogs. Keep prominently in mind the virtue of patience and the success of perseverance.

———

Don't attempt to train your dog to run beyond his natural gait by a driving system. You can get the dog to accelerate his pace, but this speed, unaccompanied by a corresponding degree of bird sense and nose, must necessarily result in the passing of birds that the dog might otherwise find, and if this gait becomes habitual as a result of driving tactics, there is bound to follow a dog of inferior bird-finding ability. In pointing dogs, the driving system also tends to produce blinkers.

———

No matter how well schooled a dog may be in the refinements of training, there is always a possibility that his natural bent will assert itself when conditions contribute to that end. The handler of a hunting dog, especially a dog with what might be described as a "mean" temperament, must be constantly on the lookout to antici-pate his dog's instinctive intent and check it before it is asserted.

———

A dog's performance at its highest water mark is the spontaneous expression of his best impulses; not the cowed gestures that have the origin in the wrong kind of training. In the expert sense, train-ing is the unfolding of a dog's instincts brought about by experi-ence, without violence of direction. Remember that a dog's best and worst impulses, which mean his instincts, are the heritage of his ancestry. Courage and fearlessness are inherited characters that may be enhanced by proper direction or marred by ill considered actions on the part of the educator.

———

It is a commonplace among sportsmen to say a dog is "beautifully broken." This implies that his training has been accomplished with-out taking anything from his natural expression. It would be well if we coined a different phrase. A trainer actually does not seek to "break" a dog; his efforts are toward educating the dog to perform in a polished manner. He wants to build the character and mold the qualities of the dog so that with true independence of spirit and inherent boldness, the canine does his work perfectly.

————

The successful trainer is the person who has a profound love for a dog. Before you undertake the education of your hunting dog, have resolved to see it through properly, not seeking short cuts and application of half measures, but with determination to accomplish the task to the best of your ability. It is well to remember the words of Phillips Brooks—*"It may be truly said that no man does any work perfectly who does not enjoy his work. Joy in one's work is the consummate tool without which the work may be done indeed, but without its finest perfectness. Men who do their work without enjoying it are like men carving statues with hatchets. A man who does his work with thorough enjoyment of it is like an artist who holds an exquisite tool which is almost as obedient to him as his own hand, and almost works intelligently with him."*

————

Lo, the poor Indian! whose untutored mind
Sees God in clouds, or hears him in the wind;
His soul, proud Science never taught to stray
Far as the solar walk or milky way.

But thinks, admitted to that equal sky,
His faithful dog shall bear him company.
ALEXANDER POPE, *Essay on Man.*

Index

Acquisition of puppy, xi, 4, 11, 53, 58
Age to begin training, 57, 61, 112
All-purpose dog, 22
American Sporting Breeds, xiii
American Water Spaniel, 4, 49

Backing, 173
Behavior on game, 161
Best lesson for puppy, 59
Biddability, 63
Bird sense, 137
Blinking, 158, 185
Bloodlines, 54
Boldness, xiv, 189
Bolting, 188
Breaking of Tony Boy, 162
Breaking Shot, 110 167
Breed histories, 13
Brittany Spaniel, 1, 23

Canine psychology, xv
Care of dog, 7
Carnivora, xiii
Character, 55, 58, 157
Check cord, 67, 87, 137, 157
Chesapeake Bay Retriever, 4, 37
Choice puppy, 51, 56
Clumber Spaniel, 2, 32
Cocker Spaniel, 2, 28
Coercion, 9, 114
Collar, 67
Come, 64, 92
Coming at call, 117
Commands, 65, 77
Competitive spirit, 179
Conditioning, 8
Conformation, 57
Conservation, x, 203
Corn-cob, 67
Crippled bird, 113
Curly-Coated Retriever, 4, 48

Dead, fetch, 129
Delivery, 122
Desire to train, xii
Development of natural instincts, 59

Driving tactics, 95, 117, 224
Down, 66
Dumbbell, 67

Early lessons, 107
Endurance, xiv
English Setter, 1, 14
English Springer Spaniel, 2, 30

False pointing, 179
Feather-Shyness, 124
Fetch, 116
Field Dog Stud Book, xiv, 54
Field outings, 59
Field Spaniel, 2, 33
Field trials, 199
First points, 98, 109, 153
Flash point, 151
Flat-Coated Retriever, 4, 46
Force collar, 68, 114
Force retrieving, 112

Game sense, 137, 138
Game shyness, 158
Genealogy, 56
German Shorthair Pointer, 1, 21
Golden Retriever, 4, 42
Gordon Setter, 1, 17
Griffon (Wire-Haired Pointing), 1, 25
Gun-shyness, 96

Handling game, 170
Hard-mouth, 125, 211
Harsh measures, 61, 71
Heel, 78
Hereditary predispositions, 60, 149
Hold, 118
Housebreaking, 73
Hunting licenses issued, 4
Hup, 84

Impetuosity, 158
Incorrigibles, 7
Independence, xiv, 9, 189
Individuality, 10, 54

Initiative, xiv, 9, 142, 177
Introducing firearms, 96
Irish Setter, 1, 16
Irish Water Spaniel, 4, 44

J.A.S.A. Force Collar, 68, 70, 76, 114
Jealousy, 175

Labrador Retriever, 4, 39
Latent qualities, 192
Lead, 76
Leaping obstacles, 214
Leash, 67
Leave it, 66
Let Go, 119
Locating game, 168

Making game, 153
Marking, 35, 123, 126, 167
Mechanical response, 138

Name, 64
Natural qualities, 5, 202, 206
Nose, xiv, 152

Obedience training, 219
Origin of dog, 12
Over-cautiousness, 181

Patience, 7
Pedigree, 55
Perseverance, 7, 89
Pheasant, 195
Physical appearance, 57
Pigeon in retrieving, 124
Pistol, 67
Pointer, 1, 18
Pointing instinct, 149
Pottering, 142, 168, 176
Prairie Chicken, 192
Prairie training, 61, 192
Precocious puppies, 51, 62, 196
Punishment, 69, 71, 90

Quail, 193
Qualifications, 5
Quality performance, 199, 202
Quartering, 134
Quick development, 197

Rabbit chasing, 190
Range, 140
Retriever trials, 209
Retrieving, 112
Retrieving specialists, 34
Ruffed Grouse, 193
Running game, 140

Sawbuck, 67, 121
Scent, 168
Self-hunting, 188
Selection, 11
Short lessons, 116
Shouting orders, 94
Signals, 93, 134
Sit, 81, 87
Sit, steady, 87
Size, 58
Spaniel methods, 27
Spaniel trials, 208
Speed, 202
Spike collar, 67
Spinoni, 1
Stamina, 202
Stanchness, 159
Starting the prospect, 107
Steadiness, 83, 155, 159, 167
Stopping to flush, 165
Style, 152, 157
Subservience to gun, 9, 140
Summer training, 112
Sussex Spaniel, 2, 32
Systematic ranging, 140

Telepathy, 143
Temperament, 9, 55
Tender mouth, 125
Trailing, 177
Trainer formula, 10
Types of points, 152

Use of sporting dogs, x

Water retrieving, 130
Welsh Springer Spaniel, 2, 31
Whip, 67, 70, 93
Whistle, 67, 93, 109, 134
Whoa, 83, 141, 157, 166

Yard training, 77